THE OTHER CHILD

Linda Scotson

THE OTHER CHILD

The Exceptional Siblings of Special Needs Children

Skyhorse Publishing

Skyhorse Publishing books may be purchased in bulk at special discounts
for sales promotion, corporate gifts, fund-raising, or educational purposes.
Special editions can also be created to specifications. For details, contact the
Special Sales Department, Skyhorse Publishing, 307 West 36th Street, 11th
Floor, New York, NY 10018 or info@skyhorsepublishing.com.

Skyhorse® and Skyhorse Publishing® are registered trademarks of Skyhorse
Publishing, Inc.®, a Delaware corporation.

Visit our website at www.skyhorsepublishing.com.
Please follow our publisher Tony Lyons on Instagram @tonylyonsisuncertain

10 9 8 7 6 5 4 3 2 1

Print ISBN: 978-1-64821-020-4
Ebook ISBN: 978-1-64821-021-1

Cover design by David Ter-Avanesyan

Printed in the United States of America

To my parents

'Love is more thicker than forget
more thinner than recall
more seldom than a wave is wet
more frequent than to fail . . .'

e e cummings

Thanks to *Ken McCarthy* for his insight
that this book should be back in print for
new generations of families and for the
efforts he went through to find a congenial
and supportive publisher. Thanks also for
his extraordinary generosity to my current
research and clinical work.

CONTENTS

Introduction to the New Edition

————◆————

When *The Other Child* was first published in 1988, my daughter Lili was twelve and my son Doran was ten.

The Other Child appeared on the heels of a previous book *Doran* published in 1985 which, through a series of happy coincidences, became an international bestseller and was translated into six languages including a special American English version (center vs. centre and other changes).

The story of Doran focused, of course, on Doran. He was born six months after his father died and had a severe case of athetoid cerebral palsy. Doctors advised me that he would never sit up unaided, walk, communicate, or otherwise interact meaningfully with the world. *Doran* was about our efforts to do what the doctors told us was impossible and ends with Doran at eight-years-old walking under his own steam thanks to the efforts of countless people including his sister Lili. If you're curious about how things have continued to evolve since after this momentous accomplishment thirty-seven years ago, you can take a peek at the book's afterword.

This book, *The Other Child*, is about Lili and is for all the children and families who find themselves in a situation like hers.

According to the most recent US Census data, over three million US children—4.3 percent of the under-eighteen population—have a significant disability. When the definition of special needs is expanded, UNICEF puts the number at one in ten worldwide and the US Centers for Disease Control and Prevention puts the number at about one in six for US children between the ages of three and seventeen.

Of course, the severity of challenges is on a broad continuum, but the fundamental issue is the same in all situations: By necessity, a child with serious health challenges requires a great deal of loving time, attention, and energy. Given that none of us have infinite time, attention, and energy to give, it is the normal, healthy needs of the able child for such things, as we all have when we are children, that are sacrificed. The "other child" gets an early, indelible, and unavoidable experience of what we all eventually learn—life is not fair.

"Why is my sibling so different?" "When will he get better?" "Why does he get all the attention?" These are questions that naturally occur in all children's minds. Additionally, children experience the same range of emotions as adults—jealousy, confusion, despair—but without the benefit of adult perspective. The challenges the "other child" faces are significant indeed and strangely, it's been hard to find books and other resources that address them which is why I wrote this book.

The Other Child is the story of how I, as a single mother, and my extraordinary daughter Lili faced these challenges and formed a team to support Doran while maintaining a healthy family life that acknowledged and addressed her needs as well.

It was not easy. It was not automatic. It was not perfect. There was a great deal of, sometimes painful, trial and error. But all these decades later, I can say that we have, by any measure, succeeded against what many people would have considered impossible odds.

My hope is that this account will bring practical ideas, insights, and inspiration to families in their own unique situations. You are not alone. Many people are on, have been on, and will continue to find themselves on this undeniably difficult path. There is a way forward and it has the very real potential of being beautiful and satisfying beyond all imaginings. I know. I have lived it.

Introduction to the New Edition

One final note: As you read *The Other Child*, please be aware that it is a historical account. It stopped with Lili and Doran at eight and ten respectively. They are now forty-four and forty-six, and many additional wonderful things have happened since then, and continue to happen.

The fundamental challenges of working with a challenged child and "the other child" in the context of family life remain unchanged. However, the clinical methods I've developed over decades working with Doran, and now many hundreds of children and adults with cerebral palsy and other serious neurological problems, including autism and seizure disorders, have evolved considerably and are described in the afterword of this book.

Linda Scotson
Forest Row, Sussex, UK

Healthcare and Social Services in the UK and the US

The UK and the US Healthcare systems appear at opposite ends of the spectrum, and a closer look is revealing.

The UK National Health Services is nationalized and offers the same universal coverage to all, regardless of social class or income. This means that things like doctors and hospital appointments, blood tests, and operations cost nothing to the individual—the whole health service, including Social Services, is paid for by the UK taxpayer.

The US model is more complicated and costs the individual money since it operates around healthcare insurance. The cheaper your insurance the more you must pay on top. In the US your family healthcare insurance may also be paid for through your job. This means that if you have a period when you are not working you often lose your healthcare very soon after leaving work.

This situation inevitably presents special problems for single parents with challenged children who wish to take on home therapy programs that need to be coordinated within their working day.

In the UK all parents, regardless of levels of income, who are carers of challenged children under sixteen years of age are also entitled to the Disability Living Allowance (DLA) to help with the extra costs if the child needs "more looking after than a child of the same age who does not have a disability." The DLA rate is between £26.90 and £172.50 (equivalent to roughly $34.15 and

$219 USD) weekly, depending on the level of help the child needs. If a parent spends at least thirty-five hours a week caring for a child who gets the middle or the higher rate of DLA they may also qualify for a Carer's Allowance. In addition, if the child is unable to walk, walks poorly, or if they are visually impaired, parents can also claim a Mobility Allowance for a car that is big enough to take a wheelchair, or which offers room for special seating.

Under the UK Children's Act of 1989, there is a general duty on UK local authorities to provide services to safeguard and promote the welfare of children-in-need within their area. The Act obliges local authorities to provide services for disabled children which minimize the effect of their disability and give them the opportunity to lead lives as normal as possible.

UK policy is that, after a child's diagnosis, parents are directed to apply to their local Social Services for a first initial assessment which will be followed over time by many ongoing assessments. All assessment is free of charge. When making an assessment, Social Services are required to "take into account the needs of the whole family, as well as that of the individual child."

UK local authorities should also provide means-tested respite care for children (also known as short-term breaks). According to the Children's Act, this care must also be of "good quality in which the parents have confidence and which ensure the child is treated first as a child and then for any disability that may require special provision."

In the US Supplemental Security Income (SSI), to help parents care for their children with mental or physical disorders, is limited to families with low incomes. Payments can help to keep families who have children with disabilities under the age of eighteen out of poverty. The SSI can cover the child's share of the household expenses for basic needs like food, rent, or mortgage and utilities. Benefits can also pay for clothing, school supplies, and other necessities.

If US parents do not receive SSI benefits, the SSI department may consider an evaluation of the parent's (including step or adoptive parent's) income and resources in relation to what is left after the bills are paid, to assess if supplementary income may be made available to meet the needs of the disabled child. This process is called "Deeming." If the remainder of the family income cannot be deemed enough to fund the disabled child's needs, the family will be entitled to an appropriate SSI monthly benefit.

In most states, children who are eligible for SSI will also be eligible for Medicare. Medicare covers basic healthcare and prescription drugs at little or no cost. It can also be used for other services considered "medically necessary" to meet the child's disability needs.

However, the US rules about demonstrating disability and income eligibility for both SSI and Medicare are complicated, and parents sometimes need a lawyer to help unravel them since it takes some work to apply for these services and to provide all the required documents. If the decision goes against a family they can appeal, but there is usually a cost involved.

In the UK, the system has proved lifesaving (often on more than one occasion) to thousands of children, including my own. However, in the longer term, although the UK taxpayer is paying for the service it remains limited to surgery, drugs, and standard physiotherapy. Other approaches, for which there are good arguments both from a restorative and a financial point of view to include, are not available. Neither is there an apparent will within the UK National Health Service to evaluate these approaches for their cost-effective potential to improve a child's quality of life.

In the US, depending on the type and level of health insurance coverage, some types of therapy that, although well-evidenced are still considered "complementary" (such as Hyperbaric Oxygen Therapy, Chiropractic Therapy, and Acupuncture), may be covered, at least in part, by the insurer. Thus wealthier US parents who can afford more broadly-based insurance plans have the advantage of being able to choose therapeutic support for their children that is costly for parents in the UK.

Both the US and the UK systems have their strong and weak

points. It also appears that neither system is independent enough of its backers to be willing to revise itself based on evidence that— beyond drugs, surgery, and mainstream physiotherapy—there lies another understanding of health and how to restore it.

Introduction

In writing about Doran, I became aware that there was a different story to be told, about a child of another type of courage, that of my daughter, Lili.

I could not do justice to both children in the same book. Lili's experiences needed their own reflective quality. I realized too that her considerable influence on Doran's life must be paralleled by other children who share their formative years with a handicapped brother or sister. The difficulties Lili faced also posed wider issues profoundly affecting families with handicapped children and which to some measure impinge upon us all.

Those who have read *Doran: Child of Courage* will know the highly unusual route I chose to help my son, and the benefits this route has had to similarly challenged children. The message of that time was clear—a brain-injured child has the clinically unaknowleged potential for true rehabilitation. Although degrees of success vary, the blind may see and those expected to become used to a wheel chair, walk. The Down's Syndrome child may become indistinguishable from her peers. Equally evident was the fact that this glorious possibility was unlikely to be taken advantage of because the treatment programme was either too costly or too time-consuming or both.

From reading old copies of the *New Scientist*, and watching a series of groundbreaking documentaries on brain plasticity, I gradually became aware that from the late 1970s, the notion of the irreversibility of brain injury had been challenged by many eminent neurobiologists. . . one of the most eminent being Professor Patrick Wall who headed the department of Cerebral Studies at University College London. The liberating possibilities of the wisdom of such potential friends in high places gave me confidence that Doran's abilities could continue to be enhanced even by a shorter programme, one that would be able to perhaps do more for all families and be much to the benefit of siblings.

Thus when Doran's time at the Institutes came to an end, we found other ways to maintain his progress which allowed us the extra luxury of discovering the long lost joys of more typical family life. . . joys which were only now available to us because of all that had happened before.

Lili is a particular beneficiary. She can now play with her brother without having him constantly yanked back to his respiratory patterning device or some other valuable exercise. She can see how all the daily hard work pays off as he charges down the lane after her, waving a muddy branch. She has also taken advantage of a shorter home programme to recover from her own problem of dyslexia which, like so many other unexplained symtoms in the world of childhood has a neurological base.

By beginning with Lili's story, I hope to enable you to identify more closely with the extraordinary problems the sibs of handicapped children live with. Their experiences take up the second part of the book. It is a tribute to them that a remarkable number survive with increased good humour and resilience. Moreover, their role in their individual household provides the crucial difference that allows each family's little boat not only to keep afloat, but to sail purposefully on. 'For the growing good of the world is partly dependent on unhistoric acts; and that things are not so ill with you and me as they might have been is half owing to the number who live faithfully a hidden life'—George Eliot, *Middlemarch*.

ONE

Lili's Story

CHAPTER 1

Lili's Brother is Born

I learned much from Lili, my first child. She showed me that simply to live can be good. That to see and hear and move are amazing gifts, and stretching out your hands to catch sunbeams and stuff them into your mouth is deliciously funny and perfectly possible.

Lili was self-assured. She educated me on the subject of babies. Now I stood in awe of the occupants of every pram I passed. On her first birthday she had been given a long blue coat embroidered with flowers. Its pointed hood and Tibetan prayer bell bounced and rang behind her, calling out to old friends and collecting new ones: 'Your daughter is an elf,' they concluded.

I was a painter. Peter had left a secure job so that the two of us could begin a new career making and restoring lacquered furniture. We had settled in a small cottage on the edge of wood and heathland.

On Christmas Day Lili waved a jester's wand. She rode on her father's shoulders while he galloped around the fields leaping brooks and singing carols. Despite his laughter, Peter was severely depressed and close to suicide.

Just after Christmas I knew I had conceived another child. Lili was thirteen months old. Her cot stood at the bottom of our bed with its side down so that she could crawl up to us in the mornings. She chatted first to my stomach and then to her own. Peter showed her how to put her ear against me and listen for the stirrings of this new personality whose growing body would be hidden for so long. The more he contrasted this solid-looking happiness with the apparently irrational despair which plagued him, the more desperate he became. By the end of March he was dead.

I collected all the photographs of Peter I could – harassing the chemist to print over-exposed negatives – and stuck them into a book for Lili. In the evenings we would sit together turning the pages of 'The Daddy Book' and some-times listening to the final movement of Mahler's 3rd Symphony which was the last music Peter heard before he died.

Lili was an early riser. She chatted merrily to herself from about 6 a.m.

'Lili, could you go back to sleep, I'm so tired.'

'I'm only talking to me, Mummy.'

'Could you whisper, darling?'

She would continue very breathily at the same volume while I put the pillow over my head and groaned.

Regardless of the difficulties, it was exhilarating to know that I had a means of earning a living for all of us. We went up to London and found commissions for work restoring lacquered furniture. The horrifying prospect of letting an infant loose amongst thousands of pounds' worth of fragile antiques evaporated as my dealers fell, one by one, under Lili's charm. She stood wonderfully still, touching things enquiringly with her eyes.

Lili and I imagined how our lives would change after the birth. The summer was warm. We went for picnics in the forest and sat with our feet in the stream dreaming of the future. Like lovers we had long enchanting wordless conversations. This was our baby and the three of us would undoubtedly thrive.

I did my breathing exercises on the bed or under the apple tree. Lili was nearly two, but she seemed ageless and timeless as she practised beside me, blowing and panting for all she was worth.

In the evenings I read to her. No matter how often she heard them, the little tragedies before the happy endings came close to breaking her heart. But she asked for them nevertheless and would never allow me to skip a word.

When she was asleep I went downstairs to be confronted by some elaborately lacquered chest or screen with decayed surfaces imploring restoration. Our tiny cottage was cluttered with the shadows of an oriental splendour, huge pieces squeezed improbably through the cottage door like genies being squeezed into bottles.

September came. One morning when Lili and I were practising breathing I felt a genuine contraction. As the day wore on we counted them together. Lili rubbed my back and blew down my neck and jumped for joy. By six o'clock I could justifiably phone Judy, a good neighbour who had promised to bring her entire family to help us.

For Lili's sake I had wanted the birth at home. Although I was over thirty my case looked straightforward. There could be nothing to worry about except the sweat and toil of the actual labour. My close friend Catherine had promised to leave her housing co-operative to manage itself and rush down from Liverpool to look after me the moment the baby chose to be born. Our excitement mounted and Lili and I sought refuge in the bath. Judy found us there covered in suds and breathing heartily.

'We're all here,' she said. 'The midwife's on the way.'

'Mummy's baby,' Lili pointed proudly at my projecting navel.

'Our baby and our friend, Lili,' I said. 'It's really fighting to get out.'

We had everything we needed. Lili produced the new orange bath tub still done up in cellophane, the mild soap and the expensive towel. She brought out an immaculate red stretch suit she had persuaded me to buy and encircled it with some of her own worn ones I had been tempted to tie-dye in orange and plum. She was unpacking treasures. She knew where everything was, she'd watched them lying there quiet and unnecessary for so long; at last they had become of the utmost value, beautiful, distinguished by their purpose. By 9 p.m., our midwife now with us, the contractions assumed total domination. Lili pulled up her pyjamas and arranged her dolls to watch. Sometimes she held my hands.

'Blow, two, three, blow, Mummy!'

I had explained that the business would be demanding so she let me concentrate.

By eleven o'clock Lili had eaten a bunch of grapes and fallen asleep. The midwife suggested some of us go upstairs and there, at ten minutes past one, Doran was born. I remember how animated and jubilant everyone was. I drew him to me with the sense that something lost was now found. There was a deep content, but also an anxiety, one I chose not to examine immediately because I had no justification and it made no sense.

The next morning Lili scrambled into bed beside us.

'Our baby,' she said.

'Our Doran.' My words reminded me of my north country roots, and I laughed. 'He's his own person too, though just now he needs us, Lili.'

'Lovely,' she said stroking his hair, 'lovely Doran.'

In the middle of all this, a removal van and three carriers arrived to pick up a large japanned chest that had taken up most of the front room. Lili ran out to wave it bye-bye. Catherine's taxi was blocking the lane, the midwife's car came close behind her. After listening to the sounds of much reversing and hooting, I slid out of bed. The party found me standing by the door nursing Doran in my arms. The midwife shooed us back. 'Lili, you're not to let your mother get up. My, your brother's very yellow, quite a little Chinaman.'

'Good Mummy,' said Lili, patting the pillows invitingly. Catherine had brought her a xylophone and she began to play to Doran, singing out all the nursery rhymes she knew. He looked towards her keenly, his eyes flashed.

Catherine said, 'He's the most alert baby I've ever met.'

During the afternoon Lili led a procession of small groups of visitors up to see 'Our Doran'. She picked flowers from the garden and arranged them in jam jars around the house and bedroom with happy concern for our comfort. She found some blackberries in the lane and brought a bowl up the stairs to feed me. We had often fed each other, like birds. Doran continued staring very hard towards us but his stare was preoccupied.

Lili had been born with her welcoming eyes wide open. We had found each other delightfully familiar. For some reason her brother was keeping his distance. The name I'd given him, 'Doran', meant 'stranger' and it was already apt.

'Lili, can you guess what he's thinking?' I said. She touched my breast and looked up inquiringly. Then she put out her tongue to lick him on the nose and stretched her arms round us.

'Sing, Mummy.'

'What?'

'Bubbles.'

So I sang 'I'm forever blowing bubbles'. It was Lili's favourite song but just then it made me unaccountably sad.

Before Catherine took her out for the afternoon, my

daughter, who was now officially Doran's sister, tucked us in and began her own medley of lullabies.

'Shut your eyes tight, Mummy.' I obeyed until she left, then I lay looking at Doran and feeling increasingly anxious about his skin colour. Could jaundice be a symptom of something more serious? Lili's happiness had such bloom to it, she was so secure. She had tried hard to be wonderful and she was prodigiously proud of her success. We had seemed on course for domestic bliss. On impulse I phoned the doctor. He was out but when the midwife came I persuaded her to test Doran's blood. The procedure was a simple prick on the heel and the results were due the following day.

Lili began to sense that something had changed. She kept coming in to look at Doran who was increasingly yellow and silent. She brought us apples and handfuls of dried fruit, saying, 'To keep your strength, Mummy.'

We were all dressed and downstairs when the news came. Doran had a dangerously high level of bilirubin, a toxic bile pigment, in his blood. He needed hospitalization fast. Lili disliked abrupt changes, she preferred to say 'bye-bye' to everything gently, but there was no time. I simply grabbed the keys and pushed everyone towards the car. The little girl's eyes were fixed on her brother, she didn't try to take a doll or a book, she came quietly and sat on the back seat leaning over the stiffening jaundiced baby in Catherine's arms.

There was an overriding urgency on behalf of Doran but my heart went out to my girl child, whose nature was as lovely as her face. I remembered a song with the line: 'To those whom much is given, much more will be required.'

Doran was snatched into intensive care. He began to have his first seizures almost immediately. Lili tried to follow him. She was brought back by the nurse: 'Stay with your mother, poppet.' We could only wait while they assessed my blood to determine what could have caused this state of affairs and what blood to transfuse into Doran, who had been given a 50:50 chance of survival: the doctors told me tactfully that there were possibilities of severe brain injury.

Lili remained rooted by the glass door to the unit. She saw Doran as her special responsibility. Since she was nearer to him in age than I was it seemed natural to her that she should be consulted. The sister came up behind me.

'There's a room for you upstairs, Mrs Scotson, if you'd like to stay. Can your friend look after your daughter?' I had never been separated from Lili in a way that prevented us reaching each other in a matter of minutes.

'We could both come early in the morning and stay until supper.'

'Mrs Scotson, this is only the fourth day after your delivery, you ought to be in bed.'

'I need to be with my children.'

'Your own health is the most important thing to your family. Please take this very seriously.'

Lili sat on my knee and began undoing the buttons of my blouse. She was very good at removing people's clothes.

'I don't want to leave you but someone has to feed Doran.' I began working my way back over the buttons.

'Me,' she said.

The sister was definite: 'Chicken, your brother has to stay with us. We'll do our best for him.'

Lili pursed her lips. There was a painful silence, then she said, 'Can I go to Lucy?'

The improvised holiday was arranged quickly by phone. Lucy was just three and didn't live far away. Catherine could deliver Lili there at once.

Lili kissed me and then went back to the glass door to cry out, 'Bye-bye, Doran.'

I was left with a responsibility to keep her brother alive and to bring him home to her safely.

A week later Doran was discharged from hospital. He was now a seriously handicapped infant – stiff, deaf and blind. He raged against this permanent night with all his energy and took succour in the only way open to him – he breast-fed voraciously. This violent life style produced acute indigestion so that when he wasn't complaining about the deprivation of his senses he was screaming with the pain of a distended stomach. I knew nothing then about brain injury, and the diagnosis of a chronic and irreversible complaint did not enlighten me.

I went to collect Lili with an old friend called 'Bert' (so called because her surname was Lancaster like the film star, although she chose to spell the name with an 'e'). Lucy's mother met us at the gate.

'Lili talked about you every day but she didn't seem to mind your not being there. How's Doran?'

'Alive and fighting, he's in the car with Bert. Where's Lili?'

The children were finishing lunch. Lili bounced off her chair and ran over.

'Mummy, Lucy,' she said putting Lucy's hand in mine as though we'd just met for the first time. 'Doran well?'

She went back to the table. 'Mummy's here,' she said to the other children, 'with Doran.' There was a faint note of triumph in her voice. She led them out to the car to meet her brother who could still pose as a reasonably substantial baby before the uninformed. Then Lili hugged everyone and waved farewell.

Our cottage was familiar but distant. We had already changed and had to begin again to make the place our home.

Before Catherine left she had taken considerable trouble to decorate the spare room to encourage me to move at least one child out of my bed. Bert held on firmly to Doran. 'Just relax, you two,' she said. The most comforting occupation we could find on that first day home was looking at 'The Daddy Book' which was also full of pictures of Lili as a baby.

'Was I always smiling, Mummy?' she asked.

'From the moment you were born.'

'When will Doran smile?'

While I was turning the pages, Bert said, 'Lili ought to have a room to herself, Linda – she's old enough. She was fine at Lucy's without you. Don't backslide now.'

I relieved her of her screaming charge and gave him succour.

'It's perfectly normal for women and children to bed down together, Bert, lots of tribes expect them to.'

At that moment Doran lurched away from the nipple he'd been gripping between his gums and howled with indigestion. I leapt up and began rubbing his back. Lili put her fingers over her ears and Bert resolutely tried another tack.

'At least if Lili has a room of her own she'll get some sleep. I suppose you and Doran will work something out.'

Lili had never been taken to bed and left awake. Our days used to interweave so harmoniously that the thought of a fixed bedtime for either of us didn't cross my mind.

'This is the moment,' Bert said, 'to establish a routine.' The little girl went happily into the pink and yellow room hung with mobiles. She listened attentively to a goodnight story and closed her eyes when I kissed her as do all good children who get kissed in books. I came downstairs and reclaimed Doran. But minutes later Lili reappeared. She crawled behind the sofa and called, 'Find me, Mummy!' Bert went into battle. An hour passed before my daughter began to recognize Bert meant business. Then she shook her golden head and stamped her foot. 'I am angry, Mummy,' she said indignantly. When she did consent to stay in her room we heard loud thumps resonating through the ceiling. Bert reported that Lili was jumping off the bed.

'Don't worry, Linda. She isn't crying, but she's a child, not a saint.'

After a significantly long silence we tiptoed up to find Lili sleeping with a doll under each arm and a picture book open beside her. Doran and I catnapped throughout the long and seemingly endless night. He was having his back patted, partly to dislodge wind and partly for human contact, when Lili opened the door.

'Doran better?' she asked curling up beside us.

'He will be, Lili, only we've got to make him want to be.'

She put her chin against my elbow and reached out cautiously towards her brother. 'If we have a good time,' I said, 'he'll feel it too.'

'Sing "Bubbles",' Lili blew softly into my face. 'Sing,' she said.

Between feeding and burping Doran and lines of song, I managed to convey the idea that we should have real fun. I knew that to pretend it would be useless. I'd thought this over very carefully in the hospital and returned to my gut feeling that life must be for learning how to love. I found myself quoting again:

> For the good are always merry,
> Save by an evil chance.
> And the merry love the fiddle,
> And the merry love to dance.

I would bless my children with happiness. Life wasn't in a book or a picture, it wasn't over the next hill, it was here in my hands. Lili was already enjoying it. Doran arched his back. His protest, partly panic, partly anger, rose to a familiar crescendo. Lili tugged the bedclothes over her head. After a moment, she threw them back.

'Doran wants tickles,' she said pulling him down from my lap and wriggling her fingers vigorously across his chest. A look of surprise passed over her brother's face. He made a new sound which certainly wasn't anger and which Lili took to be laughter. She persevered gleefully until I was dressed. Thus the discovery that Doran was ticklish made it possible for us to go downstairs peacefully and plan the day. While breakfasting on chopped apples, oats and yogurt, we made a list of Lili's friends and reviewed which ones would like us to visit them. Then she decided that it would be a lovely idea to see herself full length in the mirror above the table and stood among the plates as if this were the most normal etiquette after a meal.

'Darling, get down please.'

She waved her spoon and put her wooden dish upside down on her head. Little droplets of yogurt coursed down her cheeks and clung to her curls.

'Please, Lili.'

'I'm having fun for Doran.' She banged the dish with the spoon. It slipped over one ear and crashed to the floor. Doran and I jumped back. Before we could recover, our midwife – inevitably – walked in.

'They're difficult to control at this age, aren't they?' she said.

'Who're "they", Mummy?'

I helped her clamber down.

'If you open the cupboard, darling, we can find the dustpan.'

The midwife was followed by our doctor and health visitor, all of whom treated the house as if it were still part of the hospital. By the time our social worker appeared we were tired and demoralized.

I made her a cup of tea and determined to resist being drawn into further empty conversation. While she was shyly stirring the sugar about, Lili appeared with a large book and climbed resolutely onto her lap. As the pages opened they tipped the hot sticky liquid down the woman's blouse and into the thick tweed of her skirt. Lili had been leaning forwards and was spared.

'Are you all right, dear?' The woman set her down gently. 'It was kind of you to bring the story. When I've dried off I'll read it to you.' She patted her knee. 'Only don't cuddle too close unless you want a damp patch.' She found a towel. 'My name's Mavis. I'm going to try to be useful.'

Mavis came every week, she looked for practical solutions to our immediate problems and while she did so she was either bathing Lili or burping Doran or making me a cup of tea.

Doran needed constant pleasurable stimulation to persuade him that there was more to life than fear and pain. When I put him down, Lili took over. Once I discovered her standing in the middle of the room with her hands over her ears and her eyes shut. I waited to find out what the game was. 'I'm Doran,' she said, 'I'm Doran.'

A week after Doran was out of hospital, Lili had her second birthday. There was a large house called Oaklea in the village which had been converted into flats and was now inhabited by students of the Rudolf Steiner College, most of whom had families. The ground floor was open house and the children ran about freely, sometimes in fancy dress, invariably with sticky fingers. A message came that the house had clubbed together to provide a birthday party. So long as that community existed there was a place to go which welcomed us and where the women were ready to offer help and hope to me – and cake and mischief to Lili.

We took off each morning to visit these friends, singing in the car as it dived under the tawny autumn trees along the lane. Before the cottage door shut Lili would always jerk the last book from the long bookcase and send the whole shelf plunging to the floor. It was a piece of normal childish mischief that she delighted in. For my daughter life went on.

Our doctor had stopped coming round. He was a young man oppressed by the weight of his responsibility towards the child he'd once blithely met newly delivered into the world.

Meanwhile Lili's pleasure in her role of sister was being uncomfortably threatened by a cough and cold which grew steadily worse. I presented the doctor with this new problem in the surgery.

'Lili can't sleep. Is it bronchitis?'

'Try a little lemon and honey.'

I gave her vitamin C and a non-mucus-forming diet. She spent her nights propped up with pillows, holding my hand and choking, tears rolling down her cheeks, but without complaint. We went back to the GP.

'How's your number one child?' he said cheerfully. 'Come on, Lili, let's have a look, say "Ahh".'

Lili shook her head. 'It hurts,' she whispered.

We went away with a prescription for some throat sweets.

The coughing attacks grew worse; sometimes she simply threw herself down on the floor with her hands over her mouth. She connected coughing with pain and held back as long as possible until the mounting tempest in her chest stormed out. I unwound rolls of tissue paper for her and was aware that I was coughing myself. Lili's eyes became heavy, dark patches appeared underneath them. Her fine skin began to look grey but the little girl wouldn't give in, she took each bout as if it was something quite separate from her daily life. She wanted to get up and do things for Doran or go out, believing that the discomfort of night could be left at home. We dared not visit anybody for fear of spreading our infection. Lili found her coat with the magic bell and began putting it on. 'Darling, we can't go, you have to keep warm.' She went upstairs and came back bundled up in jerseys and scarves, then hopefully reached for her coat again. Eventually Doran had another hospital appointment and Lili was at last bewitched by a playroom crammed with toys. The consultant listened to her choking. 'That child has whooping cough,' he said.

The weather became colder. I learned how to make up the fire quickly and keep it going during the night. It was easier for Lili in the morning when she could move about; she continued to sing huskily and to look forward to Mavis coming. When I went to the Seasons, the village shop, neither Lili nor Doran was happy to stay in the car. I couldn't take Doran, who didn't appear to be infectious, and leave Lili behind. I told her, 'Lili, Doran must learn that he's safe with his elder sister.'

The shop was full and I had nearly decided to leave when Diana, the owner, abandoned her customers and came over. 'Where's Lili?' She listened to the explanation and my persistent cough, then turned to her assistant: 'A bit of a crisis here, can you take over?'

She accepted my order, adding a bottle of strengthening linctus and a bag of apricots for Lili. 'No, dear, I'll carry it outside.'

A small group of children were pressed up against the car window as though it were a Punch and Judy show. Doran had become addicted to a large purple dummy which Lili repeatedly stole from his mouth. After banging the teat on his nose she ran it gently down his cheek and back into his mouth. Doran yelled for more, the children laughed, Lili clapped her hands triumphantly then exploded into an enormous sneeze. I cleaned her up while she lay back, suddenly grey and shaking and not in the least interested in apricots. I felt despair, and turning to Diana confessed, 'Sometimes all I can think of is calling my mother.'

'Do,' she said, 'that's what we grandparents are for, we like being needed.'

My parents were anxious to have Lili as soon as possible. It was warm on the Isle of Wight and the air was salubrious. I had been given no specific treatment for whooping cough. I remembered tales of women taking their babies up to the gasworks because the fumes helped to loosen the chest. I had more faith in the household by the sea.

That night, hugging Doran to me, I snuggled up beside Lili on the sofa. 'Darling, we must all work to get well. Grannie loves you so she's coming to take you to the seaside. Grandad will make it a lovely nursing home, just for you, and Great-Aunt Mabel knows how to sing "Bubbles" and they have cats, remember?'

'Yes, Mummy.'

I made a successful effort not to cry and coughed instead.

'You come too?'

'No, I'll stay here to make Doran well for us.'

Doran was squashed and silent. I realized that he actually enjoyed our coughing; held close he could anticipate feeling the pleasantly regular vibrations coming through to him.

Lili left in a dream, her cough meant she had hardly slept for a week. My mother was a primary teacher near retirement and never overawed by professional men. She gathered Lili up.

'How could your doctor allow her to get into this state?'

'When I told him it was whooping cough he said to keep her warm and soldier on.'

'You have to do battle to get anywhere in this world,' she said. 'You fight for Doran, we'll look after Lili. You'll have her back as fit as a fiddle, but she needs a lot of care.'

I leaned against the station wall to watch them leave. A young woman with a double pushchair stood beside me. 'Twins,' I surmised. Then I saw one chair was bigger than the other. The boy and girl both had the same brown curly hair but the small sister talked animatedly to a bendy doll while her older brother lolled back, his eyes blank, his legs and arms turned in. The mother greeted an elderly lady and the two moved off pushing the pram. I couldn't bear the thought of Doran growing up like that. I resolved: 'Lili will have her brother whole, just as she deserves him.'

Now that she was gone, the house seemed to be haunted by Lili. I remembered her bathing in the kitchen sink, or the way she would suddenly appear wearing a jumble sale hat, her lips pursed like a Paris model. The dolls looked forlornly from their shelf and the books were just books, not tunnels or houses. But we had to go on. I had to make Doran believe there was a world that his senses could reach.

Then the warmth of Lili began to return; I could hear her singing, her almost unassailable optimism crept into me. Whatever we were doing we had the same faith and we were working with the same charity. I blew a kiss to her and remembered to deliver many of her soft noisy kisses to Doran.

CHAPTER 2

—◆—

Two Patients in Guy's

Days and then weeks were passing without Lili. Doran remained glued to me. A strange and wonderful change occurred. Doran's tense, desperate small body had seemed impervious to any stimulation but touch. One stormy evening I laid him on the bed as usual, and prepared to change into my night clothes with maniacal speed. Usually he screamed with might and main until he was reunited with my person under the duvet. But Doran didn't scream. Slowly, incredibly, I realized he was listening to the howling wind. The degree of hearing gain was uncertain but the happy change it made in Doran's mood and the hope it brought were landmarks in our lives.

While I was enjoying this triumph my cough became more dominating until I found it almost impossible to get out of bed. I phoned my doctor and had difficulty encouraging him to take me seriously. My friends exerted a little pressure and soon under a diagnosis of suspected pneumonia I found myself in hospital with Doran still glued to my breast.

In fact, before many days had passed, it became clear that we both had whooping cough. I didn't want to add to my parents' problems, but it was evident that they ought to know where we were. I phoned them, already forming the sentence, 'At least something's being done about us at last.' My great-aunt answered.

'Don't worry, darlin', Lili's all right but she's in hospital. There was nothing more we could do.'

I remembered the baby who discovered rainbows in the bevelled edges of the dressing-table mirror.

'Lili!' I must have roused the entire ward. 'Oh Auntie, what will I do?'

Doran was propped up in bed beside me fighting to retain his hold on my breast.

'Both your parents are with her. She's in good hands, darlin'. Just you take care of your young man.'

My head sank onto my pillows, perhaps I would lose everything.

But Doran's whooping cough slowly passed its crisis and eventually a photo of Lili arrived. She was back home with my parents now, sitting on a rocking horse; the grey drawn face with its serious expression seemed so far from the golden daughter I remembered. I turned the snapshot back and forth hoping to catch some glimpse of her familiar sparkle. My father wrote to reassure me.

'Lili is beginning to smile again. She wants to know if Mummy and Doran are getting better too. We hope that this is so.'

We were discharged from hospital at the beginning of December and in less than a week Lili returned. As she was put sleepily into my arms the promised end seemed to have been reached, no more shipwrecked seas. Excitement rose in Doran's small stiff body. The slightest shift of a muscle in him always meant something.

Lili opened her eyes and said, 'Put him in the big bath with me, Mummy, I'll look after him.'

The knowledge that his ears worked, albeit eccentrically,

30

was reason enough for her to shout loudly into them. She had enhanced her repertoire of nursery rhymes.

'Ding, dong, Doran! See-saw Marjorie Daw. It's rainin', it's pourin' on Dor, Dor, Doran!' – emptying buckets of water over him. Through the rising steam and suds Doran was enjoying himself. His mouth was open, not in a howl but in a great big grin.

When my mother left she said, 'I expect wonderful things. All the children are praying for you.'

With only a fleeting twinge of guilt in the direction of Bert, the three of us snuggled together in my double bed.

In the morning Lili pinched herself seriously: 'It is me, Mummy, I'm home. What are we all going to do today?'

We were off to a children's party at Oaklea.

'I'll dress Doran!' Lili slithered off the bed and made a beeline for a familiar drawer. As she undid his poppers in a burst, Doran lay still and gurgled. She pulled each sleeve so that his fisted hands gradually and then suddenly slid out. I had been told by the doctors that Doran would become so stiff I'd need drugs to relax him sufficiently to get his clothes on and off; these men had reckoned without Lili. When we reached Oaklea Lili practically dragged her brother over the doorstep. Doran was truly happy to be manhandled by his loving sister.

I lifted him onto my lap but he wouldn't feed. From time to time the rumblings in his stomach produced very full nappies which took us off to the bathroom. These evacuations became drier and more frequent, and nothing, so far as I could imagine, like a normal tummy bug.

Lili came home clutching a balloon. I tied it to the bedroom chair and read her a story. She fell asleep quickly, her curls tossed lightly against the pillow. The night was left to Doran who was turning slowly green and filling his nappies now with an imitation of dark brown sawdust. By midnight I was summoning the doctor. He came reluctantly, diagnosed gastroenteritis and departed to his bed. After a stressful night I phoned the surgery on the dot of nine to demand further attention. My doctor's colleague answered and advised immediate admission to hospital. So Lili, Doran and I were bounced along in an ambulance towards the Royal Alexandra Hospital in Brighton. The diagnosis now was severe anaemia and dehydration caused by kidney failure. This time Lili wasn't sent away, she had a bed of her own beside her brother's cot.

As they shaved Doran's hair and began fixing up the saline drip she rubbed her own head.

'Did you like being in hospital, Lili?' I asked.

'No, I missed the cats.'

'Do you mind being here?'

'It's different with you and Doran.'

At eleven o'clock she was still awake. We were to be transferred to Guy's in the morning; Doran had a kidney virus and needed a kidney machine.

'Guy's is in London, Lili. I used to live there once.'

She nodded, her eyes fixed on Doran, then she yawned. 'Mummy, will Doran mind if I go to sleep?' She leaned over the small still figure of her brother with the saline drip. 'Be brave, Doran.' Her eyes closed almost at once.

Doran had several seizures in the night but by dawn his condition was marginally stable and the doctors anticipated he would survive the trip to Guy's.

Lili was up early telling the nurses how to look after her brother.

'He likes baths,' she said, 'and really loud kisses.'

They helped her to dress and took her into their room for a filling breakfast of malt bread and banana.

'What can Doran have?' she asked between mouthfuls.

'For the moment all he needs is water,' I said.

'Can I take him some milk?' She eyed a bottle.

'Darling, I've got lots of the stuff and they won't let me give it to him.' I was uncomfortably full of milk and longing to disgorge it into a breast pump for some other needy infant.

'Poor Doran.'

The ambulance arrived and Doran, together with his drip, a doctor, and a nurse, plus Lili and I and a large teddy bear, all climbed into it. Lili fed her teddy bear and peeped over at her brother who lay in his own Moses basket. I was predisposed to believe his every twitch now was a seizure.

We threaded our way through a tight little maze of side streets and came upon Guy's tower block, shining ahead.

Once Lili was lifted down she skipped off across the wide marble floor of the reception lounge.

'Mummy, it's like a swimming bath.'

A group of medical staff engulfed us and drew us into a lift. From there we forged our way through countless doors to a room where Doran was attached to a new and more awesome battery of life-support systems. Outside in the corridor the Christmas decorations were being painstakingly unravelled and hung up. I had forgotten the time of year and Lili was too young to understand its significance.

They suggested I had a cup of tea. As soon as the door was open Lili disappeared swiftly, saying Doran had no toys. A small, round, yellow-skinned boy carrying a stack of papier-mâché potties which he had been commissioned to deliver hailed me.

'You lost your little girl?'

'She went to get a doll. Where's the playroom?'

'She got curly hair and a blue coat with a bell?'

'Yes.'

'She got a pretty smile. Is she stayin' in?'

'Yes, but as a guest. Lili's not ill, it's her brother who's the patient.'

He reached up for my hand and led me.

'They're short-staffed,' he confided. 'This ward is run by kids.'

Lili was surrounded by a group of children whose skin colour and slight puffiness were similar to the boy's.

'Doran's lonely, Mummy.'

'Give him Jumbo,' said the boy. He dug out a battered pink elephant from a cupboard.

They drank pretend tea with a pot and cups but Lili had a real glass of milk. I noticed that some children wore plastic bags at their waists. These contained urine not rations of lemonade. In a kidney ward pee was central to daily life; input and output were painstakingly measured. The playleader came over to ask me to slip off and see the consultant. Lili handed me the elephant. 'For Doran,' she smiled. 'Come back soon, Mummy.'

'I will, darling.'

As I walked down the corridors I saw that even the doctors went down on their knees to hug their small patients. The consultant was warm and sympathetic. 'Parents are very much approved of here,' he said, 'but you must find somewhere else for your little girl. Do you have any friends in London?'

The kindness at Guy's was plainly evident but I had stumbled upon a rule and there was no arguing my way out of it. The registrar touched my shoulder. 'She still has a nasty cough, probably exacerbated by the central heating. I'm sorry there's nothing more we can do for you.' He paused and muttered almost to himself, 'Unless she gets worse.' Then he turned abruptly and disappeared into the ward.

I phoned my friends Theresa and Peter Marinker. They

had a son, Daniel, a year older than Doran and a year younger than Lili. Theresa agreed to come but it would have to be immediately. Lili and I were given approximately half an hour before adjusting to another separation.

We had visited Daniel two weeks after his birth. He had seemed so at home with us that Theresa decided to take a bath. Daniel watched her go and then remembered he was hungry. Without standing on ceremony he began to nurse from me. Lili dropped the bricks she was playing with and came over to watch. The idea became appealing and the moment Theresa returned she climbed confidently onto her knee and put a small hand down her blouse.

Daniel's father was an actor who could tell terrible tales about witches and demons. Lili would run round the room fighting them until they were all thoroughly dead . . .

Theresa arrived at the hospital on time. Lili and I kissed as though she was off on an afternoon outing; I was as trusting as she was. Despite everything, or perhaps because of everything, Guy's had a magical quality.

The following afternoon I was hurrying back to Doran's room when the registrar caught me. 'Congratulations,' he said, beaming, 'your daughter has just been admitted. She's in the next ward, now you can just breeze between the two.' He'd put Lili down as 'suspected pneumonia'. The condition had developed overnight and worsened by midday when Peter and Theresa brought her back. I found her sitting up in bed showing all the symptoms of a heavy catarrhal cold but otherwise cheerful. 'Mummy,' she said, 'Daniel's walking!' Then she sneezed. We all rushed to provide her with tissues.

I wiped her nose and kissed her cheeks. 'Oh Lili, I did miss you. It's so good to have you, we'll have a wonderful Christmas. They always are in hospitals.'

'How's Doran?' she said.

'At least he hasn't got a cold.'

'I know, Mummy.' She sneezed again.

Lili's room looked newly carved out of concrete, it was painted bluish white. She had an assortment of toys and games and a nurse almost to herself. The inconvenience was that 'suspected pneumonia' meant isolation.

If she stood up on her bed and peered through a small glass window she could just see the child in the adjacent room, a bonny baby recovering from whooping cough. Here was an image of the normal development intended for her brother. I marvelled at the delicacy of his hand movement and the way both eyes opened wide to watch his mother when she fed him. Lili studied the baby playing in his cot; the movement of his own body provided him with unlimited opportunities for recreation. She turned. 'Does Doran like Jumbo?' I had forgotten the pink elephant.

'I'm sure he does, darling.'

'Because he can't find his toes to play with, Mummy.'

The nurse arrived bringing the antibiotic. Neither the presentation of the two drinks in tiny milkshake glasses, nor the colours, one orange and one yellow, could overcome their sickly smell which I could hardly stomach. Lili pounced on them, drank them both down with enthusiasm and licked round the edge of each glass. This was probably the most sugary food she'd ever had.

I ran, more like the wind than the breeze, between both children, but it was soon clear that Lili needed other visitors if she was to stay happily ill for an indefinite period of time. The Marinker family decided to go to Cambridge for Christmas. I was wondering who else to phone when the nurse brought in a visitor.

'Linda, Lili, this is my hospital. Why didn't you tell me?'

It was Clare, an educational psychologist who had once been our neighbour. Clare seemed to have acquired detailed information about us from other sources. 'I thought you'd be thirsty, Lili, so I brought you some Perrier water.' Lili's eyes indicated that this was absolutely right. Clare poured a beaker full and turned to me. 'She has sophisticated tastes, our Lil.'

Clare also brought some colouring materials and a drawing pad. 'She and I are going to cover this place with pictures, aren't we, Lil? You go and take our love to Doran while we carry on with it. I can come in almost every afternoon. Get along now.'

When I got back the patient was asleep, and a great many of her painterly abstractions covered the walls. Clare said, 'Once she'd finished up the paper she wanted to set to work on the furniture, "Like Mummy does". When I'd talked her out of that idea she began on me.' She rolled up her sleeve and presented an arm richly embellished with felt pen.

I walked back with her towards the room where Doran lay steering himself between life and death. When we got to the door she peeped through its small window, hesitating.

'Do you want to go in?' I asked.

'No, I can't bear it. Linda, don't you think it would be for the best if . . .?'

'If what?' I had forgotten how many brain-injured children Clare had seen.

'You have to think of Lili's life too, you know.'

'I do. What do you mean?'

'She's such a bright young thing and you have such a good relationship. I don't like to think what may happen. Doran could suck you up . . . Perhaps I'm just a coward.'

I knew how much Lili loved her brother and it was hard to believe that he didn't have something to give her. Gifts like beauty are often in the eye of the beholder, so who could blame an outsider for being scared?

Lili's visitors increased. I found her sharing her tea with a French painter who had never spoken more than two words to a child in all the years I'd known him. He came back the following day with one of his etchings and a small box of oil pastels '*pour ma princesse*'.

We were urged to spend Christmas and the rest of our time in London with the playwright Bernard Kops and his wife and family, all of whom knew Lili well. In fact they were the first people that Peter and I had told of my pregnancy. Bernard had dangled a ring over my tummy.

'If it swings to the right it's a girl,' he said, 'or is it a boy? Erica,' he called to his wife, 'do you remember?' She didn't. 'Ah then,' he said, 'you've got either a boy or a girl.'

Peter smiled at that. 'She dreams continuously of giving birth to a cat, sexually indeterminate, a bright orange Persian with magnificent blue eyes.'

Bernard's fiftieth birthday was a month after Lili's and at his party his guests had pounced on the one-month-old Lili.

'This is the most social baby I've ever met,' exclaimed an actress with a famous husky voice. 'Did it come by itself?'

I put down my glass of champagne as Lili leaned across towards me. I said, 'We have a special relationship and I think she wants a drink.'

Peter caressed my neck. 'Lili can always find her mother,' he said, 'she has a very good homing device.'

The Kops had last come to see us over a year ago in springtime. We took them into the bluebell wood. The tall green stems held a blue lake which reached beyond Lili's waist. She still asks to return to the flower pool which will never be quite so wide and deep again.

'Lili is a lily but her eyes are bluebells,' Bernard said.

I explained about Christmas carefully to my mother over the phone.

'Couldn't Lili come here?' she asked.

'Mummy, we love you but we have to stay together. Doran needs us and I need Lili. And she knows how important she is just now.'

'We're all worrying about you but that's not much help to you at the moment. We want to do something.'

'Darling, your time will come,' I said, 'believe me.'

Doran achieved the impossible; as though as a seasonal present, he got off the kidney machine by Christmas Eve. The registrar scratched his head. 'We'd expect him to be three months on dialysis even if he'd nothing else to bother him. What's the secret? I wish I could give it to all my patients.'

Lili was up and well by Christmas Day and Clare came for Christmas lunch. She brought an array of delicacies, including smoked salmon. 'For us,' she said, 'as hors d'oeuvre, but Lili could try some.'

Lili was given a small slice. She ate it with such ecstasy we couldn't resist giving her more until our hors d'oeuvre had become her main course. After lunch I carried Doran about locked to my breast and sucking continuously. Lili had the radiance of a prisoner restored to the world. At six o'clock we left her brother asleep in a real bed. Hand in hand we took the lift to the ground floor; snow was falling and the taxi drivers were charging double fare because it was Christmas, but we rejoiced.

'Doran won't be lonely now, Mummy,' Lili said. 'The other children told me they'd look after him.'

Bernard met us at his door and drew us in, brushing the snowflakes from us. Lili sat on his knee to eat a mince pie.

'I thought you'd be thin and wan, my Lili,' he said, 'and we'd have to tempt you with warm gruel.'

'What's that, Mummy?'

'A sort of soup,' I said, 'for invalids.'

'Did Doran have it?'

'With salt, in a drip.'

She put down the pie and began to wrap a bit up in her paper serviette.

'Is that for Doran, Lili?' Bernard asked.

'Yes.'

He helped her tie it up with ribbon and gave her another.

We took our first bath together since Doran's birth. His children doubled up and gave us one of their rooms with its posters and puppets and landscape china ornaments crossing the dressing table. A mushroom house night-light glowed securely beside us on the floor. The bed was quite narrow so we slept curled up together like a cat and kitten.

We were due at Guy's in time for Doran's ten o'clock feed which meant leaving by 9 a.m. Opening the door hardly provided an invitation to go out. The snow had been piling up and there was ice on the pavement. Erica Kops began dispensing woollies. Lili buried herself in cardigans and knitted hats, so that it was difficult to squeeze her coat on. She had been given gloves fastened to a string and thick socks but there were no boots to fit. This didn't worry us unduly until we began the journey up the road to catch the train. It was only a few hundred yards, but actually getting there without slipping or being blown over demanded team work. We clutched each other close and zigzagged from the kerb to the wall. There was little respite at the Underground station which was now transformed into an iceberg poised at the top of perilously frozen steps. When we emerged we were faced with the descent from a footbridge hung with icicles. I bent down in the snow, Lili climbed onto my back and slowly we came down this Everest.

We arrived at Guy's reception with a great sense of achievement. The gulf stream of its central heating enveloped us. Once in Doran's room I could strip Lili down to the clothes which were dry and put the rest over the radiator.

Lili had been right about the other children, Doran was now the object of great curiosity. The doorway blossomed with chubby faces. A very articulate young lady of eight had a powered wheelchair which she drove at reckless speed.

'Would your little girl like a ride?' she asked me. Lili indicated she most emphatically would. The two of them set off down the long corridor of tinsel and fable, jamming on the brakes beside a large pile of unclaimed toys that half a dozen charitable Santas had left.

Lili's life on the ward gave her freedom to indulge her curiosity about lifts. More than once she was returned by a nurse.

'I found her going up to Men's Surgical, they'd love her but . . .'

To Lili, pressing buttons or slipping in behind someone taller who could take her to greater heights was like finding worlds on top of the Faraway Tree. Reasoning with her could be difficult, mainly because she was disarmingly honest.

'Lili, will you promise not to do it again?'

'That's too hard.'

The best solution, authorized by the ward sister, was to keep the heavy double doors leading to the lifts shut, thus retaining Lili firmly in our more prosaic territory.

Wherever we went we carried a running picnic of black bread, cheese, nuts and fruit. Lili perched on the end of Doran's bed and bit into an improvised sandwich before informing me: 'Those poor children have to eat things they don't like.'

'Could you offer them some of yours?'

'They're not allowed.'

'Why not?'

'They can't have . . . I don't know.'

She paused and then ran off to ask the girl in the wheel-chair. She came back and took a deep breath. 'Mummy, it's the Pot-ass-ee-um and the So-di-um.'

I found out that cheese was high in sodium and fruit was high in potassium. The evil-smelling grey stuff they actually did have was some kind of meat stew. If Lili had needed any further inducement towards vegetarianism the sight of it would have been sufficient. 'Your brother's lucky to have milk,' said the girl in the wheelchair.

Lili nodded, 'Mummy makes it.'

As we talked, shadowy feathers of snow caught against the window, darkness was drawing in and the journey back to the Kops would undoubtedly be worse. Then Moe, an art history graduate and companion from my student days, who'd been a regular visitor of Lili's already, appeared. He proceeded to propose miracles by offering to carry Lili to and from Guy's every day. To demonstrate his reliability he lifted her onto his shoulders so that she could reach the Christmas decorations.

'Can Doran try?' she asked. Doran found himself swung upwards amongst the gold and silver balls which dangled from the ceiling.

'He's smiling,' Lili was emphatic. 'He can see them, I know he can!'

However incomplete his vision, Doran now hankered for shiny things which Lili gleefully made it her mission to collect for her frustrated magpie of a brother.

Moe trudged through the snow morning and night to deliver us to and from Guy's. He soon concluded that unwrapping Lili from a large bundle of snow-sodden woolly garments had its disadvantages. He steered us persuasively into a chain store to purchase a child's zip-up warm waterproof suit. Since Lili's experience of shopping for clothes was almost exclusively at jumble sales, she treated the expedition with almost religious awe. She stood so still when she tried the suit on I was convinced she couldn't move.

'I think it must be too restricting. Lili, can you turn round?' She remained rooted to the shop floor.

I sighed, because the thing was lovely. Then, with great presence of mind, Moe dived behind a rack of coats crying, 'Lili, I'm being eaten by a crocodile! Help!' She flew to him, Moe sat up and looked in the direction of a fierce but retreating reptile.

I said, 'It won't hurt the suit if you walk about in it.'

'It was made for chasing wild animals,' said Moe.

By the time we set off once more into the snow Lili had grown accustomed to the fact that she didn't have to keep as still as a tailor's dummy in a shop window.

As Doran's kidney function grew steadily better, the ward became a rendezvous for my good-natured bohemian friends. Moe proposed that we all take Lili out to a restaurant. The consensus was that the Hari Krishna Vegetarian Curry House off Charlotte Street would be the most appropriate. We were quite a bunch: two painters, an engineer, an art historian, a dancer, a psychiatrist, and Lili. Everyone ordered her a small portion of their own favourite dish and there was much competition to discover which she liked the most. Lili plunged in without fear; each serving seemed more delicious than the last.

'Are you doing all right?' Moe asked.

'It's lovely.'

But the cumulative effect of the spices had yet to be brought home. After a good twenty minutes she stopped suddenly and whispered, 'Mummy, my mouth hurts.'

She took another spoonful of dal and opened her eyes very wide. 'Ouch, ouch, ouch!'

I offered water but it had little effect. Moe suggested yogurt and a huge bowl of it was whisked onto the table by waiters. Lili ate it with serious application. Halfway through she took a deep breath.

'Better?' I asked.

'Yes, thank you.' She frowned suspiciously at the remaining bowls of vegetables. 'More yogurt, please.'

When the day came for us to leave Guy's, Lili had a large extended family genuinely unhappy to see her go. Moe swore he'd come down often and the children on the ward promised to write, but to Lili it was like parting from a foreign country.

'I'll never see those children again,' she said tearfully. 'Never, never, never.'

'Perhaps one day when you've grown up, Lili. All sorts of things can happen.'

A hospital car delivered us to our cottage door. Judy and her family promised to shop for us because the snow and ice was still thick and my car was marooned. I knew how much I would surely rely on Lili throughout this winter which barred our door as effectively as the hospital isolation barrier. I could keep us warm by blindly ignoring the impending fuel bills. I could provide the form of our entertainment but it was Lili who would be its spirit. She would make us merry and ward off the evil chance.

Although this homecoming was a victory, Lili and I now had to face the actual problem of Doran's brain injury and what to do about it.

CHAPTER 3

——◆◆——

Lili's Role Changes

Lili hated the cold. I tried to clean out the grate and make up the fire before she woke so that the room would be welcoming. For this exercise to be efficient Doran had to grit his gums and put up with being in a baby sling instead of my arms.

One morning when Lili was rummaging in her toy box she found the old baby bouncer.

'For Doran?' she suggested. (Doran was normally always carried.)

The bouncer fitted to a hook in the ceiling and suspended Doran upright with his feet just touching the floor. He was small enough to be quite well-supported even if he slouched. His own mechanical jerks activated the spring and he bounced up and down on his feet. More purposeful assistance from Lili introduced him to an entirely new experience.

'Like this, Mummy, I remember.' She twisted the cord, Doran pirouetted.

As we brought him gently to a standstill his pupils seemed to go on revolving.

Lili looked at them with all the expertise of one who had studied the oracular mechanisms of dolls.

'Will Doran's eyes have to go round inside his head to come back, Mummy?'

The pupils, still at variance with one another, slid into

45

view; Doran was happily turned in the direction of the fire which must have had all the visual appeal of a field of comets.

We were cut off from the every day world as much by Doran's condition as the weather. Lili's instinct to invent became an asset. In the mornings I'd hear her stealthily opening drawers, then she'd leap upon me wearing, for example, a pair of pants on her head and a waistcoat down to her ankles. She didn't often bother with the mirror, she had the knack of knowing exactly what she looked like just by the feel of the clothes. She always succeeded in making me laugh and laughter was particularly useful because it stimulated Doran and kept us all warm. I knew my DHSS money would not pay the heating bills. I assumed it must be more economic for them to pay the death grant.

One day I remembered baby massage; I had a book, *Loving Hands* by Dr Frederick Leboyer. Lili scrambled onto a chair and found it on the bedroom shelf. We put a towel on the bed and a bottle of olive oil to warm by the fan heater. Lili, rapturously, reduced Doran to nakedness.

I poured some of the warm oil onto her hands.

'Work slowly up the arm,' I said.

She looked longingly at his tummy.

'Can I start there?'

This was not the order of the book but it delighted Doran. When we'd finished one side she said, 'What about his bottom?' and we turned him over. She was also good with toes. Bit by bit we believed we were introducing the body to its owner.

Our belief was innocent but tenacious.

Lunch was usually eaten with appealing pleasure by Lili and rather less reverently by me because Doran insisted on dining at the same time. Breast-feeding my desperate child was better achieved with two hands so that he had more than simply the suction of a limpet to hold him in place. From time to time Lili pushed a fingerful of cheese sauce into his mouth and took great satisfaction in seeing it returned clean. I was never sure whether Doran's main interest was in the texture of Lili's finger or the taste of the food because he refused all my offers from a spoon.

I washed up with Doran's body tucked under my left arm so that his head and fists projected over the sink. Lili pretended that my right arm belonged to her and when she gave the order it would obediently swab down the plate she held up. When all the possibilities of entertainment at the sink were exhausted we went back upstairs to enrich our frontiers in the spare room, with the valiant aid of the old and noisy fan heater. Lili had to be persuaded not to smother this appliance lest it cut out for ever allowing the DHSS an easy victory. Her idea of a satisfactory degree of heat was only reached when she came out in nice red blotches. We shifted slowly round the room as I tried to entice her away from the heater, but she had the ability to be continuously on top of it without any visible sign of having moved.

Lili had accumulated hordes of coloured bricks of varying sizes from every possible jumble sale. She made it her responsibility to build towers and Doran's to demolish them. This was impossible for her brother to achieve deliberately, but occurred as an ungovernable response to her performance.

She erected columns nearer and nearer to him until his back suddenly arched in excitement, his arms and legs shot out and bricks avalanched over us as a consequence.

'Well done, Doran!' she'd say pouncing on him and shaking his hand. He visibly puffed up with pride. She made him feel that his body had some innate and automatic ability to be successful.

In the evenings we painted in front of the fire. Lili poured her whole self into the activity, spreading out the colour with a brush and rubbing it in with her fingertips.

She thrust a brush into Doran's fist, wiping her own fingers clean down the side of his stretch suit, and pushed his arm towards the palette. The brush stuck out from his clenched hand like a sword projecting from a toy soldier. Once douched with colours, it made contact with the paper, spreading out its bristles and leaving a crude rainbow in its wake.

'Mummy, look, he can paint!'

Doran had a grip which was not, unfortunately, combined with an ability to let go. The paint brush, like the red shoes in another fairy tale, would have remained glued to his hand for ever if Lili hadn't removed it so that he could use his fists instead. When I towed them to the bath, still dripping with paint, I wondered whether to put them both in without bothering to undress them to economise on the necessity of washing their clothes separately.

I rarely looked at the clock. When Lili yawned we went up to bed and she cuddled Doran while I read her a story. Then Doran would be exchanged for a bear or a doll and I'd wander about the room patting his back and humming nursery rhymes to his sister until she fell asleep.

January and February slipped away. Judy and her family brought us food and nappies and budgeted for us, because I had no idea what was in or out of season. Lili was often able to find apples in the shopping but oranges or bananas were rare gifts from foreign lands, as was the post which brought cards and letters from the Isle of Wight. There was enough to do and sufficient humour in the doing of it to ensure our survival. Lili didn't worry about the future; we had put all our energies into defeating winter.

One day Mavis, our social worker, arrived and asked what we were going to wear when spring came. Lili tried on her beautiful coat and noted with horror that the arms were now nearer to elbow length. Had the coat shrunk? she tried stretching its sleeves. Then she said, 'It doesn't matter, Mummy, we can keep it for Doran, when he's well.'

But where should she get a new coat? Mavis suggested the WVS rooms in Lewes. They had a stock of clothes and blankets for the 'worthy' poor, and she could drive us there to make our choice. After all, Lili needed tights and dresses as well as a coat, and what about me? I thought I might have too individual a taste in clothes for the WVS.

Going out in a car was a holiday. Lili appeared fascinated by all moving things outside the window.

'Look, Doran,' she turned his head from side to side, 'cars, cars, cars.'

We arrived at a large Georgian house and trailed through its long dim hallway to a series of rooms, each more like a wardrobe than the last. Nothing seemed to be an exactly appropriate size but Lili loved all that the two motherly women in charge thrust upon her. The things were folded into neat little piles and put into carrier bags.

The highest shelf was stacked with knitted blankets in many chequered colours.

'Does she have enough on her bed?' one of the women asked. 'Poor mite, the weather's been very cold for you.'

I opened and shut my mouth wordlessly, unsure of the degree of destitution which entitled one to blankets.

'They're very special, we have an old lady of over eighty who makes them all the time. We can't stop her.' They began parcelling some up. They brought me a tweed coat which I was destined to wear gratefully for the next three years. It was difficult to find something for Doran and I realized that we weren't actually going to be allowed to leave until he'd been catered for. Then Lili discovered a pair of blue bootees in a tea chest, which satisfied everyone. We thanked our benefactors and took the spoils off to Mavis's car.

At the end of March the thaw came overnight.

'The sun's warm, I can feel it,' Lili said, as she leaned against the window frame and pressed her hand on the glass.

I opened the front door and stepped out onto the crazy paving. The snow had shrunk into tiny crescents under the hedge and the smell of earth rose softly into mild spring air.

'Winter's over, Lili, we've won. Soon the leaves will be back on the trees; they uncurl like little hands.'

'Will Doran's?'

I gave her one of his small neat fists and she wound back the fingers and put her thumb into his palm; the fist snapped shut over it.

We walked along the farm track to the car. Lili thumped it affectionately as though it were Doran.

'Wake up,' she said.

I'd dressed her in a long yellow mackintosh from the WVS and a pair of wellington boots which fitted with the aid of several pairs of socks.

'Where are we going, Mummy?'

'To buy you proper shoes. Grannie sent the money ages ago.'

The car choked, puffed and spluttered. With a great deal of nursing it managed to get out of the lane and onto the main road. Doran sat in his car seat holding Lili's thumb in his hand.

We drove victoriously into East Grinstead. The manager of the rather posh shoe shop looked taken aback at the intrusion of a bunch of cheerful gypsies. Lili climbed up onto one of the children's chairs and I summoned an assistant who removed her client's large boots to reveal small feet in green darned socks. Doran chose this moment to have indigestion and needed to be thumped.

'It's all right, Mummy, I'll do it.'

Lili left the foot measure and laid hands on her brother who, once recovered, looked for a reviving drink which I was not really dressed to provide.

Shoes were brought, but they were too tight. Doran struggled frantically across the front of my coat. Then Lili unexpectedly announced that she needed the toilet quickly. She was unused to its being anywhere out of reach.

'Could my little girl please . . .'

They weren't insured, their toilet was only for staff. The nearest Ladies was three streets away.

'Lili, can you run?' I asked.

She shook her head. As I was struggling in the direction of relief, with Lili on my back and Doran under my arm, we passed another shoe shop with a picture of the Start-Rite boy and girl in the window.

'Mummy, try here!' By good fortune she'd chosen a shop where the use of a toilet was all part of the service. Furthermore the smart blue shoes fitted and Lili went out wearing them.

We celebrated the event by visiting a couple who taught at the Steiner school to which many of my friends sent their children. Vicky and Jeremy lived in a caravan in the grounds. Lili ran out to play with another small girl under school age. I watched while they dug in the sandpit and pushed each other on the swings.

Then I showed Doran the painted Easter eggs that hung across the caravan window. He tried to reach them but his arms were too tight and he remained boxing close to his chest. A rising fury of frustration broke from him. When I looked back towards the sandpit Lili had gone. I searched

for her under the rhododendron trees which led back up to
the school hall. She jumped out behind me. I at least was
easy to locate because of the noise from Doran.

'I've found a baby, come and see,' she said.

Doran and I followed her through the bushes to where
her friend was waiting. The child's front door was at the
bottom of a clock tower with stairs so steep and narrow
Lili went up on all fours.

'It's a magic baby,' she whispered, pushing me into a low
room, its pale slanting ceilings draped with rose-coloured
silk. The baby lay in a white wicker cot under a canopy
of pink and violet veils. We tiptoed closer, a soft light
shimmered mistily over the perfect, sleeping child. Lili
said, 'Don't let Doran wake her, Mummy, she might
disappear.'

I put my hands over Doran's mouth and withdrew from
the room. The children's mother met us in the kitchen.

'I've heard about Doran,' she said softly, stroking his
hair.

'He likes it if you shout,' Lili explained.

'Does he hear?' said the woman. 'I wondered because he
has wonderful ears, musical ears.'

On the way home Lili said, 'I don't think I'd like Doran
to be a magic baby.'

'Why?'

'Because I couldn't tickle him.'

Then she said, 'Why didn't that lady look at my ears?'

'I think she was only interested in babies,' I answered.

At the beginning of April, our friends Judith and Michael
came back from America. Having chosen to become god-
parents to both children while Doran was hale and hearty
and as yet unborn they were anxious to catch up on their
now more disturbing responsibility. When Catherine
arrived for Easter we all proposed going out on a picnic

together. Michael had discovered a pleasant beauty spot behind their house. Getting there entailed carrying Doran across a ploughed field and a fallen log over a stream.

We eventually arrived on a grassy isthmus made by the meander of the stream. Having washed off the mud from our encounter with the field, we spread out the cloth and began to unpack the food. At this vulnerable moment we were engulfed by a herd of cows.

'That one's got Doran's hat.' Lili reached after the grey crochet cap Judy had made to protect his precious head. The large Jersey cow was prepared for a tug of war.

'Leave it,' I yelled.

Lili paid no attention. She hung on until the cow opened its mouth to complain. At last she had the initiative and most of the cap.

'I'll put it back now.' She looked at my anxious face. 'Mummy, we do have to look after Doran.'

The spring wore on and we did our best to see that something was always happening to Doran. Sometimes Lili just shook him to make him happy. She would say, 'Doran needs attention' (people were always telling me that he must receive a lot of it), and go to work.

We were sitting under the apple tree which had just started to blossom and Lili was busy giving Doran 'attention' when our health visitor arrived.

'Is she safe with the child?'

'He enjoys it,' I said.

She raised her eyebrows. 'Come on, Lili, let's have a look at your brother. You're a little stiff today, Doran.' This was an understatement and she knew it. Doran couldn't lift his head up. His eyes rolled about everywhere, usually lodging like two half moons on either side of his nose. His hands were fisted. Whatever his intentions, the only gesture he could produce was to arch his spine furiously. This eliminated any hope of my squeezing him into the seated posture except in the car seat and endangered my teeth from the impact of the back of his skull.

'I think he's pretty desperate,' I said. 'Surely there's some treatment you can offer?'

'Oh Doran will be all right, he's not lost much weight.'

'But he's not *doing* anything. Imagine what it must be like for him.'

'I think he's content enough in the circumstances.'

Lili chimed in, 'Doran needs help, doesn't he, Mummy?'

The health visitor smiled.

'I expect you want your mummy to yourself, Lili?' She turned to me. 'You don't leave them alone together, do you?'

'Lili is Doran's most stimulating friend.'

'Well, be warned, dear. You were an only child, weren't you?'

Lili went off to get the yogurt pots and some water to make mud pies. Doran lay on his stomach and started to howl. It was a new and fearful grief as though the full hopelessness of his life had suddenly struck him.

There had to be some change. When Lili came back we were alone. 'That woman was wrong,' she said.

'About what?'

'She doesn't think I can help Doran get well.'

'Lili,' I said looking at the overflowing yogurt pots with sudden inspiration. 'You always have known the right things to do with Doran. Would you like to go swimming, almost right away?'

It was a hazardous business managing two children in and out of the water – Judith and Michael had now flown back to America and I could think of no one free enough to help us in the pool – but from that hour swimming became a daily feature in our lives.

Later in the week I had a phone call from the Secretary of the Tunbridge Wells National Childbirth Trust.

'Hello, Linda, we're in a bit of a quandary. We thought you might provide a solution.'

'I'll try.'

'We've had a plea from an American girl who wants to come to our classes. She lives with her boyfriend and we think we'd be much too middle class for her. You had two natural childbirths, your experience might be valuable.'

Being middle class or otherwise couldn't really relate to breathing exercises. After some reflection I concluded the more appropriate word would have been 'conventional'. I guessed by now I didn't seem entirely conventional to anyone. However, Frances appeared on our doorstep to find Lili waiting to teach her.

'I've heard,' Frances said, 'that the best thing to do is to go swimming. Do you ever drive to the pool?'

I burst out laughing. 'All the time, Frances, all the time.'

Lili invariably showed initiative. On the days when we didn't see Frances we drove to the Crawley pool. Since I never actually swam but merely walked about in the water propelling Doran on its surface as if he had an outboard motor, I was always shivering. If Lili was out first she stood with her back flattened up against the wall in front of the changing rooms. She would edge along it very slowly as if it overlooked a precipice. At last she recognized my plight.

'Didn't you know Mummy, it's warm here.' She patted the wall. It was, I discovered, a huge radiator.

I snuggled close to her and pressed Doran's bottom against the penetrating heat. He smiled broadly and began to pee. Once, Lili couldn't be found. I tried the usual places like the men's changing room in vain. I was about to persuade a lifeguard to drain both pools when I heard she had been retrieved on her way up to the cafeteria.

'Do try not to run away,' I implored as I hugged her.

'But I'm always safe,' she said.

It wasn't worth going home for lunch if we went to Crawley, so every evening we would pack a picnic ready for the morning. Lili found that the door next to the pool led to a crèche with slides and a climbing frame. She decided to go there in the afternoons while Doran and I had a second swim. When the weather was fine we ate sitting on the grass in the playground. There were other women with children who soon discovered the nature of our daily life and looked sadly at Lili.

'She must get a bit jealous, he takes up all your time.'

'Do you give me what they said?' Lili whispered.

'Do I what?'

'The jelly stuff.'

'Oh jealous, that's a feeling, you can't eat it.'

'Can Doran?'

She had run off back to the swing while I was still thinking of an answer.

On the way home we passed a farm which sold yogurt. Lili's job was to leave the DHSS milk coupons on the ledge in the dairy while I exchanged empty pots for full ones. She never forgot. Afterwards we'd go down to the barn where the cows were being milked. There were tricycles outside and wooden toys. Lily looked wistful.

'Where are the children?'

'At school, Lili.'

'Can I go to school?'

'One day, Lili.'

'Can Doran go with me?'

'One day, Lili, one day.'

Her brother's state of mind was better. At eight months old he clearly felt that things were happening. There was a daily pattern of change that he could anticipate. He wasn't bored. But he wasn't actually doing anything for himself. He couldn't turn his head or play with his toes or roll or crawl or sit up, although he could now be successfully forced into the seated posture. He could see but with eyes that either locked into the corners by his nose or wandered about without reference to each other, I had no idea *what* he saw.

We decided to visit Judy's family on the way home. She had the ground-floor flat of a rambling old red-brick house where she grew vegetables and kept hens. One of my landscape paintings hung over the divan. Lili studied it seriously.

'I wish we could live there.'

'We do,' I said.

'No Mummy I mean really *in* one of your pictures.'

'Would she like to feed the hens?' Judy asked.

Lili was given a dish of corn and went outside. Doran and I wound ourselves into an armchair and Judy enquired, 'How's junior?'

'There must be another way of reaching him. The capacity is there, I'm sure of it,' I said.

'In the meantime you'll kill yourself gadding about with him. Lili's the one you should be worried about, Linda. She looks tough but underneath she's frail. That chest!'

'I understand what you mean, Lili's sensitive but she does have strength.'

'I wouldn't be too sure. . .'

That night when my daughter was asleep I carried Doran round the bookshelves hunting for a file. A month after Lili's birth a friend had arrived unexpectedly for tea waving a copy of the baby's astral analysis which she had commissioned from a consultant astrologer.

Lili's father was as much scientist as artist and advised caution. We read the document, politically forgot the contents and hid it away. I retrieved this piece of history from between Peter's dusty copies of Tolkien and lay down on the sofa with Doran in the crook of my arm.

'Listen, my son,' I said. '"Lili has the sun in Libra, the moon in Taurus and the ascendant in Pisces . . . there is tremendous artistic potential in this combination. Her pathway may lead down subterranean tunnels lesser mortals would fear to tread."' Doran then indicated it was time that we walk round the room again and I paced about, balancing the book on top of him. 'There's pages and pages: "Her basic nature is gentle, sweet, compassionate and kind, so how will she handle the intensity within? An artistically creative outlet is the obvious one and she should be given every opportunity to develop in this way."'

Doran lurched backwards and I lost my place. At the top of the next page were the words: "She will suppress her own needs if she feels others will be offended, thereby engendering a sense of guilt."

'We've got to look after your sister, Doran. Promise not to be unreasonable in your demands.'

As if he had perfectly understood, Doran now unfailingly went to sleep in his cot downstairs when I put Lili to bed and dutifully stayed asleep until I had finished reading her story. As soon as I was back in the kitchen with my hand extended towards the kettle intending to make a cup of tea, he woke up, vociferously reminding me that I was to be shared.

At the end of May the Rudolf Steiner teacher training college, where so many of my friends were students, had its Festival. We took an afternoon off swimming. The young sunshine pressed its warmth into the folds of our cotton clothes. Lili wore a homemade jumble sale dress which was cream with green ribbons threaded through the sleeves and hem, and daintily smocked.

The college lay set back from the village on a terraced hillside. Jesters and clowns were darting about distributing paper flowers. The children all wanted them in their hair, but Lili made sure that Doran's were tied round his sun bonnet. A May Queen riding a white horse appeared with a procession of her courtiers. All healthy athletic figures, they danced round a tall garlanded pole. When the music began again it was the children's turn.

'Mummy, can I dance with Doran!'

Even the fittest seven month old baby cannot skip round a maypole unsupported so both Doran and I joined her as she wound in and out among the other children until we were face to face with her again. She planted a kiss on her brother.

'Doran is my prince. Oh poor Mummy, I'll find one for you.'

She turned and raced off into the crowd with a purposeful expression on her face. Doran and I fled after her. We pushed onwards through the carnival and rediscovered her talking to a tall sandy-haired man with a Siamese cat on his shoulder and two children tugging on his hands. The woman beside him exclaimed, 'Hello, my name's Alice. Lili just grabbed my husband for you. I think she'd like to hang on to him for a while – he's taking the kids to the puppet show.'

The man departed with the children and cat in tow.

Alice went on, 'I've heard a lot about you. I'm a healer, I'd like to give Doran what I can.'

She belonged to a religious community called White Eagle Lodge.

'Do come, and bring Lili too,' she said.

I'd been to healing services before. My own religion was founded on my instincts, surely there were more things in heaven and earth than science would ever make clear?

I explained to Lili that Alice would try to help Doran heal himself.

'When you cut your knee a plaster keeps the wound clean but your body is doing the mending.'

'Why can't Doran's mend?'

'He's trying to make it when he's yelling his head off, but the message doesn't get through. If we could persuade more blood to flow to the part that's hurt perhaps it would begin to get better.'

'Will Alice talk to Doran's blood?'

'I think so,' I said, feeling slightly out of my depth since I'd produced the explanation on the spur of the moment.

Alice collected us, drove over the top of the forest, turned down a long track through the trees and parked outside a graceful old house.

The gently-spoken grey-haired woman who came out to meet us was introduced as the priest. We shook hands and proceeded up some stairs to the chapel. Then she took Doran over to the altar and Alice put her hands over his brow and began to pray. Lili immediately raced in and out of the lines of pews and stood on a kneeler to get a better view of a Madonna and child. It occurred to me that I ought to restrain her but the priest said: 'She can run about as she likes, the chapel is to be enjoyed.'

Lili called me to look at another painting.

'That little boy has stars round his head.' She paused. 'Let's go and see Doran.'

We stopped a few yards behind the altar.

'Stay here, Mummy.'

My skin began to glow.

'Can you feel anything, Lili?'

'Yes, tingly. What's going to happen now?'

One afternoon in early June, Judith and Michael were back in England and invited us to tea on their lawn after swimming. This time Judith had an extraordinary piece of news. It concerned a clinic in America called the Institutes for the Achievement of Human Potential. Its director and staff believed that it was possible to reorganize the uninjured part of the brain of a handicapped child to take over fully from the part that was injured.

'It's our destiny to go there,' I said. 'All I have to do is find the money.'

Judith laughed.

'You can start with buying the book by its director, Glenn Doman. It's called *What To Do About Your Brain-injured Child*, and it's published by Jonathan Cape.'

I read this book in one night. Doran must have sensed I needed to because for the first time in his life instead of short dozes, feeds and demands for stimulation, he slept. The next day I began to explain some of the ideas to Lili.

'Doran needs to learn to crawl, most babies crawl before they walk.'

'Did I?'

'For ages and ages, once you got used to the floor. Before that we used to travel around cheek to cheek until one day things lower down began to fascinate you.'

'Like what?'

'Patterns on the carpet, bits of fluff, tins of tomatoes from the cupboard. I started to live on the floor with you. We rolled tins of tomatoes under the chairs.'

'I don't think Doran will like it by himself, Mummy. We'll have to all go down there.'

She was of course right.

Fortunately a friend of Judith's called Diane Phillips, who had worked at the Institutes and was Judith's main source of information, intended to stay in England later in the spring. She would supply us with all we needed to launch the huge enterprise that would commence Doran's real road to recovery. I knew people would worry even more about

Lili. In some ways she was an unusual child, but weren't all children unusual? She taught me that herself. Could we combine our special intimacy with an intensive programme and the number of helpers I would need in the house to move her brother's limbs in the cross-pattern motion that would at last enable him to crawl?

CHAPTER 4

— ◆ —

Love is Not Enough

October 9th was warm and sunny. Lili had her birthday party on the lawn at Judith's. As she fed Doran his piece of carob cake, Lili said, 'I wish you'd have another baby for us, one that wasn't brain-injured. We'd like a playmate, wouldn't we, Doran?'

'Wait till you and Linda get helpers,' Judith encouraged. 'You won't be doing this on your own, you know.'

'They'll be grown up.'

'Not all of them – the mothers will bring their children.'

'Little ones?' she asked dubiously.

Our appointment at the Institutes was confirmed for the New Year. Lili had accurately predicted that the floor would not be to Doran's taste but there was now a fundamental rule that he should be on it. Appreciating his need for mobility, she towed him about by the heels. Despite the daily increasing gap between Doran and his outgoing, ever active peers, I was optimistic. The floor programme had already improved his head control. He could keep his chin off the carpet enough to look at a picture book. I have no idea what he actually saw but he manifestly enjoyed the experience, I didn't question where my energies came from and I was not prepared to give up.

It was difficult but even more essential to keep cheerful as the nights drew in. The outside world grew colder and the daily plunge into the public swimming baths less and less appealing. An invitation to use a Cheshire Homes hydrotherapy pool from 5 to 6 p.m. appeared to be an unexpected godsend. We set out optimistically, following the map on the seat beside me.

'I'm hungry!' Lili said for the tenth time as I found myself caught up in yet another ringroad of early rush-hour traffic. The snack I'd brought for her was under the dashboard. I groped for it earnestly while I prepared to signal. 'I promise we're nearly there!' I found the small packet of cheese and raisins at the next traffic lights.

We arrived and changed, Lili carried the red potty to the side of the swimming bath to take care of emergencies. She launched herself from the steps. The next moment she was taking off her arm bands and slipping gracefully below the surface.

'I can swim!' she choked as I hauled her to the side. The temperature's remarkable similarity to her domestic bath had banished all consideration of depth. I explained the necessity to keep afloat in order to breathe, and replaced the bands. Both children grew pink and shed their worldly cares, they had made a temporary return to the balmy days of amniotic fluid.

At home I returned to the theory in Glenn's book. Well babies develop their brain growth through increasingly sophisticated physical activities. To encourage the unin-jured part of a hurt child's brain to take over the functions that have been lost he needs to have these movements patterned on to his own body while he lies passively on a comfortable table. The simplest 'patterning' I could find required only two people, one to rock Doran's body from side to side and one to turn his head. I read that it needed to be repeated at least four times a day if the stimulus was to have the required effect of creating new neural pathways in Doran's brain. Several good friends elected to help me. Margaret, my next-door neighbour who was fond of Lili, came in every morning to pattern Doran on the breakfast table.

'What colour is my pullover, Lili?' she asked. 'Red,' said Lili.

The garment was brilliant green.

'What colour is your potty?'

'Green.'

This went on every day, fuelling Margaret's growing conviction that Lili was colour blind.

Then one morning Judith arrived with a large box of subtly toned shade cards.

'See if I can tell the difference,' she said to Lili. 'It's extremely difficult – will you test me?'

She proceeded to give so many wrong answers that Lili irresistibly corrected her.

'Why don't you play like that with Margaret?' I asked. 'You've got every one right.'

'Mummy, it's a different game.'

As winter approached, my nights walking the boards soothing Doran, coupled with the need to press on regardless, made the gaiety a little forced. Lili saw I was tired and preoccupied. Without drawing attention to herself, she slipped into a secondary role. Imperceptibly, with each day that passed, I was beginning to lose sight of her. I longed for sleep but Lili longed for me.

Towards the beginning of December she caught a cold which went straight to her chest. I stoked the fire while she lay on the sofa covered in blankets.

'How do you feel?'

'Fine,' she whispered.

'But, darling, you look so . . . so . . .'

'So what?'

I kissed her but I was afraid. We had a new doctor. When he came he asked the same question, received the now ritual and almost inaudible answer and prescribed an expectorant for her cough. Our most recent friend, Brenda, whom we'd found working on a nearby farm, came round offering help.

'You're not so well I hear, Lili.'

'I'm fine.'

Brenda smiled. 'Just like your mummy.'

'What do you mean?' I asked.

'That's what you always say when people ask. However tired and ill you look, you always grin and answer "I'm fine".'

Overnight Lili's temperature rose sharply. By morning the sheets were soaking in a mixture of her perspiration and melted ice from the cold compresses I was still applying with shaking hands. With the doctor's promised arrival came the diagnosis of pneumonia and a swift and eventful flight to hospital. My world was now concentrated upon Lili's oxygen tent. Doran was whisked away to become the guest of Judith and Michael.

At last I had nothing to do but love Lili.

She had insisted on abandoning any night clothes.

She wriggled her toes, 'It's like when I was a baby and you were always smiling.'

When Lili came out of the oxygen tent we slept together in the low bed I had occupied beside her. We woke slowly. 'I dreamt I was inside you again,' she said.

The strength returned to the arms she so often entwined round my neck. By the time she was climbing the furniture, the hospital, almost reluctantly, discharged us.

Close to Christmas Judith and Bert founded a benevolent fund to send Doran to America. They planned the initial stages of our campaign to raise £1,000 in two months.

Lili and Doran stayed with my parents while I went into hospital to correct a prolapse that had lately frustrated my spontaneous dancing and made me wary of sneezing unless I was sitting down.

During my convalescence at Judith's the rest of the money was raised.

Brenda elected to go to the Institutes with us. Judith was travelling over a few days earlier and would meet us in New York to drive us down to Philadelphia.

Before she left she introduced me to a young woman called Magda Shlenkier who decided she'd spend her holiday by coming too.

I had been away a month when I went alone to collect the children from my parents' house. I hesitated shyly in the doorway clutching a push and go lorry, and wondering if I had become a stranger who must wait patiently for recognition.

I bent down to greet Lili and felt her rush warmly into my arms. I knew then that all we gained was still there as fresh as ever. I promised myself that I'd never, never lose it again. She slept with the lorry on the pillow beside her. We held hands across the twin beds, with Doran, now weaned, on a mattress on the floor in the middle. The next step was our flight to America.

Once we'd trooped through the mirrored reception lounge, the hotel in Manhattan became unashamedly shabby. But since this was the only hotel of Lili's experience, she rejoiced as loudly as though it were the Palace of Oz itself.

'Are you American?' she asked a middle-aged lady waiting for the lift.

'Sure I am, sweetie, where are you from?'

'From England.'

'Would you like to go buy yourself some candy?'

She thrust a coin into Lili's hand and disappeared into the elevator.

'Mummy,' Lili whispered. 'Doran will be all right because people give you money in America.'

We travelled to Philadelphia with Michael and Judith, arriving at the Chestnut Hill Hotel in the dark. Once luxurious, it was now rundown and much kicked about by the homely presence of hundreds of brain-injured children and their brothers and sisters. At last we were only a short drive from the Institutes. I was as excited as Lili, but given the chance, more capable of sleep.

For these initial weeks we knew that Lili was going to be the only sibling. Normally first evaluations were so hectic that it was the one time when the presence of well brothers and sisters was judged inappropriate.

The programme of work we received was heavy but we'd expected that. We would be living in a way that would change the future to which every doctor had apparently condemned us. It struck me that no matter how much the Social Services might have worried about Lili since she had become the sister of a handicapped child, there was no back-up system to help children like her. They were neither acknowledged for the work they did nor given the support and understanding they needed for a home experience that made exceptional demands on their characters. The Institutes, on the other hand, were offering advice and help to the family as a whole.

Lili shared Doran's progress from assessment to assessment, and her questions were answered with affectionate respect.

'She's very unspoilt,' an English staff member, Mike Downey, remarked to me after watching her giving elocution lessons to the Americans. 'Somehow I thought she would be spoilt.'

Lili came over. 'He speaks English. Will Doran speak English or American?' This was an interesting point.

Lili had been caught up in Doran's anticipated wellness. She repeated the things we had to do, all the way to Kennedy Airport. Then she kicked off her shoes and skipped around collecting a pocket full of 'lucky' pebbles from the potted palm trees in the departure lounge.

Doran's programme is described at length in my book *Doran: Child of Courage*. We had fifteen five-minute patternings which were intended to induce Doran to crawl 1000 feet in a day by the time we returned to the Institutes in three months' time, when we were all due back for a second evaluation. He had a breathing exercise lasting one minute which was to be repeated sixty times a day in order to increase the depth of his respiration, develop his chest and pattern his brain for good, deep breathing. This meant placing a small plastic mask with a narrow air outlet over his nose and mouth. Breathing in a higher level of carbon dioxide than oxygen triggered the breathing reflex; he drew deep strong breaths and continued to do so after the mask was removed. Lili could share Doran's well-organized reading programme necessitating the continual production of groups of flash cards with large red stencilled words. She helped to explain what we were up to at a series of meetings and newspaper interviews. Her good nature was inspiring; in a week we had gathered three months' supply of kind interested people who could give us their time. The day was broken up into three sessions of two hours each, and in between these sessions I carried on with the masking and the floor programme and produced meals.

Lili stood on a chair beside me while I patterned. We felt close to each other while her brother belonged to the world and had become in a sense separate. She put her hand on my hand and together we manipulated Doran's leg or

69

turned his head. Then she stamped and shouted and clapped, urging on her 'horse' as at last he forced himself slowly but surely inch by inch across the linoleum. The children who came played the same game until they went away for lunch or tea. This was certainly fun and the results were very evident. But the inflexible routine coupled with my having to drop everything and mask Doran every seven minutes if he was to get anywhere near sixty maskings in a day began to affect her. She took away the mask I was using and ran outside across the lawn.

'Lili, can I have it?'

'No.'

She had never said 'No' in so memorable a way before. I hadn't the time to register shock, I simply grabbed another mask and carried on. Lunch needed to be on time. There was a large ball with a reverberating bell I'd put a few inches from Doran to encourage his progress while I sliced vegetables. Lili came back and picked it up.

'That's lovely,' I said. 'Will you shake it a bit in front of him?'

'No, Mummy.' She was off again, this time with the ball.

The vegetables went into the steamer. I seized another toy for Doran and masked him again. I knew I should chase Lili round the garden and laugh and kiss and carry her back on my shoulders, but the importance of time to fool around had been driven underground. Even lunch was curtailed — it was so late that we were obliged to leave the last of it when our patterners arrived. I was aware of having ignored my three-year-old teacher. I made an effort to suppress all irritation in the hope that it would diffuse away, which of course it did not.

Lili did not always say 'No' but from that point onwards I knew I couldn't rely on her saying 'Yes'. I could see Doran was making the first real progress of his career, and I knew

70

the heavy prejudice that surrounded this treatment which was his life-line. Every domestic problem we had would be a chance for the programme's detractors to condemn it as unworkable. There were no official provisions for supplying the family help I so desperately needed. I had stuck all of our necks out, it was my responsibility, but if success were to have a price then the price ought to be a fair one.

Soon the children who came to see us were entirely familiar with the performance. They rushed in to take over. This rowdy atmosphere was an advantage for Doran, but his sister began snatching the toys out of their hands.

'No, those are Mummy's,' she said protectively. 'Mummy's books, Mummy's toys.'

'They're not mine, Lili,' I reproved gently. 'They're yours and Doran's.'

'You bought them, Mummy.'

'Lili, these children come here to help. We need them.'

Lili ran off towards the swing; immediately a small boy overtook her. She went up to him and shook the seat.

'It's my go.'

'I was here first.'

Then the rest of the children crowded round demanding their own turns. Soon a tug of war was in progress. Since this turbulence stimulated Doran in the right direction my instinct was to make light of it.

'Well done, he's covered ten feet now. Apple juice everyone!'

The children scrambled back leaving Lili thoughtfully swinging to and fro by herself.

'I'll come later,' she called.

At night in bed the strain lifted and there was a temporary transformation in our relationship. While Doran sucked sleepily at his bottle, Lili and I had a résumé of the events.

'What do you like best, Lili?'

'My goodnight story,' she said.

'What about the children?'

'They're all right, but they won't play with me. They're here to do Doran.'

I wished I could give Lili something that was her own. I could only praise her volubly in the hope that she would recognize how much I appreciated her.

'Let's go to Grannie's,' she said stroking my cheek.

'Maybe, next year.' I tried to be realistic. 'We'll dream about it instead.'

'I'll try. Can I have the story about Mr Rabbit and the Birthday Present?'

The change in Doran continued to be heartening. Everyone, even my health visitor, had noticed it. We were nearly two months into the programme, the weather was unusually hot and Doran had just completed the impossible feat of crawling up over the back doorstep and liberating himself on the linoleum donated for the yard.

It was lunchtime and I was about to bring out a picnic for us. Fatigue had engulfed me.

'Lili, could you get your little chair?'

'No.'

'Please, we're on time, we can really enjoy the sunshine!'

'You do it, Mummy.'

I flushed with anger and hit her sharply on the leg.

'Lili, do as you're told.'

The red patch on Lili's skin and the echo of my screeching voice were stupefying evidence that I'd not imagined the incident. I knew I hadn't slept for more than a couple of hours together at night since Doran was born. I had nothing to fall back on.

'Lili, I'm sorry, I'm so sorry.'

She didn't utter a sound, she stood very still while I kissed her. This unhappy scenario was repeated throughout the week; I was growing addicted to getting relief at Lili's expense. The discrepancy between night and day in our relationship became unbearable. At last, instead of raising my hand, I left Doran to make his own way across the kitchen floor and took my daughter on my knee.

'Lili, I shan't ever hit you again. I did it because I was tired and confused, you've spoilt me. I love you and I'm sorry.'

'You need attention, don't you, Mummy?'

'Lili, I know Doran won't get well unless we help him. I'll try and make things better for you. I really will.'

She licked my tears. 'You taste nice.'

After a few days in which my sense of humour and Lili's optimism were comparatively restored, the plague of 'flu which had swept the village singled me out as a ripe target. One evening I found myself on the floor unable to get up. In some desperation I crawled in a rather inferior cross pattern to phone Magda, who used the remaining days off work due to her to come down to nurse me and take over the programme. After fighting a way successfully through her first day of organized chaos she exclaimed, 'Linda, you cannot cope like this – you need a CSV.'

'A what?' I murmured uncomprehendingly from my sick bed on the sofa.

'A Community Service Volunteer. It's a charity that sends young people out into the field to help families in need. It will be wonderful for Lili.'

After two weeks of negotiations, Nancy walked through our front door. She was a warm Yorkshire girl with plenty of dry humour and a perfect way with Lili. Why no one had told me about this life-saving organization before defeated reason. I hadn't left the house for nearly three months – now I could risk taking my patterner's advice.

'Go for a walk with Lili, we can cope; besides, there's Nancy.'

Sunlight twirled in the leaves of the aspens which lined the drive to the riding stables across the way. Lili decided to climb the gate and see the horses. We kicked stones and drew with sticks in the red clay soil.

Nancy shared Lili's imaginative world, she cooked and cleaned and mothered us and we adored her.

Lili's relationship with Diana at the local shop, the Seasons, had grown as close as if she were a god-daughter. I didn't belong to any religious denomination, but I'd been told that the Rudolf Steiner Christian Community had a baptismal ceremony which was essentially a welcoming of the child onto earth. Diana consented to become a god-mother and Peter Marinker, who I knew would take Lili's interests completely to heart even if it meant fighting me, agreed to be her godfather.

Gradually other people began responding to Lili's social needs. An artistic looking lady proposed inviting us both to supper on Tuesdays at six. We followed a trail of toys from the front gate to the dining table. The disarray was unbeatable for its colour and texture. Lili learned that she liked avocados and how to peel artichokes and dip them in garlic butter.

Nancy took Lili to playschool.

'She's very quiet,' she reported. 'Not at all like at home.'

Lili said, 'Can Doran come next time?'

'He has to wait a while yet.'

'But Mummy they won't believe I have a brother!'

We returned twice to America and the Institutes over the summer. Doran's programme evolved. He acquired a method of patterning his respiratory rate which would further improve the oxygen supply to his brain. Lili was intrigued by the small sleeveless jacket, made of canvas, which had straps crossing his chest and extended to wooden dowels. While Doran lay on his back on the patterning table, two people sat on either side of him gently pulling on the dowels in time to a specific beat of the metronome.

'Pull, hold, release,' Lili chanted faster and more enthusiastically, I had to beg her to stop in order to keep time myself.

Doran had graduated to steeple chasing – crawling over low obstacles, which was intended to help him rise up on all fours. He also had a vast range of categories of flash cards with clear pictures on the front and names printed carefully on the back to give him new information which would encourage his brain to grow. This involved much cutting up and sticking down. Lili's own production of cards for Doran emerged in a stack; since she found scissors difficult she made her categories from off-cuts. They had rather subtle connections, if Doran ever becomes a poet I shall attribute it to her.

Many of the children we met went to the Steiner playschool. I felt that if Lili met them there, in a different atmosphere, the friendships which she longed for might come naturally. Our introduction to the playschool looked optimistic. The room was pleasantly shaped, more like the inside of a nut than a school. All the toys were sturdy and made of wood. As I watched, the children held hands with their teacher, making a big circle, which Lili was invited to join. I left hoping that the welcome would be real and lasting.

Christmas passed, Doran rose onto all fours and pulled himself up into a standing position.

Nancy had left in early September, and Cathy arrived to replace her. Now that we had found CSVs we had a security but we had to adapt to change. In early spring Alison, a biology graduate, arrived. She came in like an electrical storm and could hardly sit down before she was leaping up again peppering me with significant questions.

'Lili, this is Alison.'

Lili said, 'Doran's creeping now. Will you read me a story please?'

She pressed a book into Alison's hand and held her in place by sitting firmly on her lap. She explained about Doran's programme.

'He does it all the time, Mummy never goes to bed and we all have to be on the floor.' This was said as if it were some kind of treat.

The next morning the temperature was still freezing. Doran spent long periods on the floor so under his jersey and trousers he wore two sets of stretch suits, with part of the arms and legs cut out of them.

'Mummy,' Lili called, 'Alison's in a muddle, I'm helping her.'

Alison was an intellectual who had never studied the theory behind dressing children. She had fastened both the stretch suits on upside down and put them over Doran's other clothes, not underneath. Lili also showed considerable talent when it came to demonstrating the delicate job of holding Doran still while one put on his nappy – she sat on him.

The relationship between Lili and Alison was between two equals. It drew us together, although I noticed that the more secure Lili felt within this enlarged family the quieter she became outside it. Whenever she was taken out for tea she increased her reputation for being in a dream. I began to discover that much of Doran's programme and therefore her home life contradicted Steiner's philosophy which postulated that reading should not be attempted before the age of seven, and that children shouldn't be exposed to pictures of things they hadn't actually encountered in their own lives. It was also held that all toys should be made of wood which was natural; plastic was viewed with suspicion. So far the people I had met who valued Steiner did not take these opinions dogmatically and I knew that the philosopher himself believed that since every situation was different, one should use one's intuition and make up one's own mind. I found a great deal in his work beautiful and kind and I had been persuaded to invite a kindergarten teacher over to discuss Lili's future at the school. The sofa faced a favourite powerful painting of my own which vibrated with repetitive flourishes of green, red and black. As chance had it this now clashed violently with a strip of lurid blue lino, donated for Doran's crawling. The teacher attempted to avert her eyes, and later expressed a highly charged opinion of the harm done to children brought up in violent visual surroundings.

'Do you know that Steiner feels that young children like your daughter should only paint with pastel tones? She shouldn't see too many paintings – a Madonna perhaps, the Raphael is very good. Do you have a Madonna?'

At this moment Lili and Doran arrived naked out of the bath. It was seven o'clock, Doran's programme was far from finished and Lili was patently not tired.

'How nice,' the lady said, 'I have caught them before bedtime. Goodnight, Lili.'

While I was debating whether or not to gag Lili and rush her upstairs she said irrepressibly, 'We were only having a bath to get rid of the crawling dirt,' and then before my despairing smile she produced a mask and Doran's flash cards. 'Can I see them, Mummy?'

The elastic was ripped off. Presidents of the United States, dinosaurs and extravagant adjectives fanned out onto the living-room floor while Alison innocently placed the transparent plastic mask over Doran's nose and mouth.

The lady seemed not to believe what she saw. 'I think,' she said, 'I have caught you at an unhappy time.'

Alison had little idea of Steiner's teaching and she elected to read *The Lord of the Rings* to Lili as a bedtime story.

'Stop if it frightens you,' I warned. 'She can read something else.'

'It doesn't, but when will the good people win?'

'They don't always, Lili,' Alison said. 'But they will in this book, you have to be patient.'

When the chapter was finished Lili said, 'Doran's always good, isn't he, Mummy?'

'No, he's a mixture.'

'He can't help crying because he's brain-injured,' she protested.

When both children were finally tucked up and asleep Alison mused, 'If I'd had a brother like Doran I'd have murdered him by now. He's very lucky. Why doesn't she hate him?'

'He makes her laugh,' I said 'Besides which she's a very caring person.'

'Don't you wonder if she's not *too* good? She could be seething underneath and we're blind to it.'

After the next trip to America, overhead ladders sprang up in the house and garden. Doran began walking underneath them while Lili and our patterners' children climbed on top. Doran's progress went on late into the night and Lili pleaded for a temporary bed for herself to be rigged up by the ladder so that she could fall asleep in our company as soon as she was tired.

On the eve of Easter Alison watched while I decorated the kitchen with painted eggs and dyed and hard-boiled them for the old Lancashire custom of egg rolling. I ground various mixtures of fruit, nuts and spices, shaped them into eggs and decorated them with tones of toasted coconut.

'You are a miserable killjoy,' she said.

'Why is chocolate better?'

'Because children like it once in a while.'

'Don't you even think the room looks pretty?'

'It's not the same as a big egg in shiny paper.'

'But Lili doesn't know about that, chocolate doesn't tempt her.'

'Because Doran's on a diet it doesn't mean that Lili has to suffer it too. Don't be such a precious parent.'

'Oh Alison, I felt sure Lili would have a surprise.'

She threw her arms impulsively round my neck.

'Don't listen to me.' She picked up an egg and crammed it into her mouth. 'Actually, they're delicious.'

Next morning Lili ran into the kitchen.

'Mummy, the fairies have been in the night, come and see!'

We rolled the hard-boiled eggs ahead of Doran like footballs, and then ate them one by one as they smashed against each other. There was a wild sense of rebirth. We played Mahler's 'Resurrection' so loudly we had a phone call from the neighbours, but it was the last Easter without Big Eggs in Shiny Paper.

Lili invented more extraordinary games to induce Doran along his outdoor ladder. She and Alison rigged up the hose pipe so that it provided a fountain at the end. To this Lili added a series of buckets and pipes, allowing the water to run into the wheelbarrow where boats could be floated and thence into an old baby bath in which she could paddle. Soon afterwards a climbing frame arrived on loan from a generous patterner. Within seconds of its appearance Lili was standing fearlessly at the top like an elf who had just jumped out of the apple tree.

'Mummy, look at me!'

She had taken off her clothes and her bare toes closed

round the tubular steel bars. A child of nature, I thought, although the fact that she couldn't actually fly provided a less comfortable edge to my admiration. Alison cried, 'Stay there, Lili!' and ran for her camera.

During the warm and strangely humid summer most of our time was spent in the garden. I looked forward to Peter and Theresa Marinker arriving with their family. By now we thought Doran's ladder walking impressive and Lili's custom of skipping about the garden without clothes and playing the hose pipe on anyone less appropriately undressed nothing if not charming. This vision faded before the reproving eyes of our visitors. I was, after all, asking a two-year-old boy to walk endlessly up and down under an overhead ladder day in and day out, and his sister to put up with a household bent on encouraging the lunacy. Nevertheless, Peter suggested that Lili come and stay with them the following weekend.

The day he came to collect his godchild there was considerable difficulty in persuading her to dry off and find decent clothes. The insect bites she had on the top of her thighs had turned into a rash which yielded neither to calamine nor Anthesan. Lili didn't seem unduly worried but they looked unpleasant and, I guessed, uncared for despite the battery of creams.

When he brought her back the atmosphere was equally difficult. A few days later a letter arrived.

'I think you inhabit a world where there is little proportion and your well-meaning friends have been offering the wrong sort of support. It cannot be right to spend such enormous amounts of time and energy on Doran. Your life and that of your daughter are, *if anything, more important than his.*'

I knew that if we neither put Doran in a home nor murdered him, the pain of watching him atrophy daily in

his wheelchair would have been unbearable to both of us.
But the letter frightened me. I saw the writer's integrity and
would defend his right to comment. At the same time,
I was hurt and miserable and wanted sympathy. I
was finishing breakfast. Doran was already on the floor.
I kept re-reading Peter's words, hoping to find something
I'd missed to reduce the impact. Alison expressed anxiety
and I pushed the page over to her – it was impossible to
explain . . .

'His intentions are obviously good,' I said. 'I suppose I
chose him as Lili's advocate and I'm only getting what I
asked for.'

'Peter ought to come and stay here for a month,' she said.
'I don't think anyone can judge what happens on a day
trip. I've changed my mind countless times but I can see
Lili's happy and she does genuinely enjoy Doran.'

But before the end of August Alison's own future gave
cause for concern. The grant that she needed to do research
hadn't come through. Lili bestowed comfort, often going
up to the bedroom where her grown-up friend lay, moody
and depressed. They developed a game of talking to Alison's
feet which had a more philosophical view of life than their
owner. Lili hated anyone to be seriously sad. She worked
at finding a little thing intricate enough to turn the sufferer's
mind in another direction. I knew she used the same knack
with herself.

Doran's goal was to walk two steps unaided by his ladder.
He was at last regularly stepping out into Lili's arms.

'I can catch him,' she cried. 'I'm strong, come on, Doran,
we'll get to America.'

She had stayed with my parents during the previous trip;
now both she and Alison would be there to help us. We
found the clinic resounding with the exploits of well and
hurt children alike. Friendships were quick and warm. In a

lecture, Glenn had talked about not leaving your wounded on the field of battle. This philosophy seemed quite natural to the sisters and brothers who changed nappies, timed masks, delivered vitamins and generally larked about with their brain-injured comrades. The atmosphere was an invigorating combination of idealism and realism, and made me wonder how the world could ever be presumed to have sunk far from grace.

The new programme meant exclusive ladder walking except for three weeks when Doran would be whirled about in all directions to help his balance.

Lili had just moved from my bed into her own room. She was unlikely to be lonely since Doran and his vestibular activity had moved in with her.

'Do you mind living in a fairground, Lili?'

'No, but it's for Doran – I don't fit anything.' Doran was spun upside down from a hook in the ceiling, spun on an office chair, and spun on a wheel fixed to a huge board against the wall. He was also rolled backwards and forwards between us.

'You need a real fairground, Lili, but your teddy would fit. Shall we try him?'

Lili was now nearly five years old. Although I had heard nothing from the education authority, my friends began asking which school I would choose for her. Having her spend the best part of every day away from home by law was almost shocking. I had resented my own primary education because of the degree of conformity it imposed. I knew that directing the business of learning so that it was always fun entailed hard work on behalf of the teacher and I had always entertained the illusion that if I had any children I would send them to a different sort of school – or no school. Lili, however, woke up one morning insisting that she go to the local village school. She remembered it from the summer when we used to take Doran there to crawl and she had tried out the small desks and admired the show case of stuffed animals in the corridor.

The school had recently acquired a new headmaster. I had no idea what his policies were but I phoned up the day before her birthday. Without any preamble she was given a place. Alison was delegated to acquire Lili's uniform, lunchbox and satchel. She rushed back with these acquisitions which were wrapped up as extra birthday presents.

So Lili set out for school as though she was going to see Peter Pan on Ice. It was an unusual birthday treat from the state. I lingered at the classroom door while she disengaged her hand.

'You're sure you'll be all right?'

'Yes, Mummy, don't worry.'

Lili stepped into the room, turned and waved goodbye.

CHAPTER 5

---◆·◆---

Friends and Critics

I hoped that this new school would give Lili the chance to make friends of her own age. Adults loved her, her real friends were all grown up. Had she missed being a child? Had she been encouraged to think too little about her own needs?

'At the moment I'm just letting her play,' the teacher assured me.

Once when I went to collect her I peeped in through the side window. The class was scurrying about in circles tidying things away, only Lili remained standing at her desk, like a child who'd been turned into stone by the Queen of Narnia.

By the time I'd reached the door the spell had broken.

'Come and see my teacher, Mummy!' I followed her with my anxious question: 'Has Lili any special friends I could invite home to tea?'

The teacher shook her head.

'You see she doesn't conform. At this age children don't usually like being different but Lili seems not to mind . . .'

We drove back to our cottage with its overhead ladders leading from front gate to back garden and ducked under them to get inside.

Sue, the freshly resident CSV, had been walking in front of Doran reading him *The Cat in the Hat*. He hurried the last few feet to greet Lili who opened her lunch box and extended the sticky remains of a half-eaten pear.

'Mummy, can we have Doran's music on?'

I played the tape of Joan Armatrading singing 'I'm lucky I'm so lucky, I can walk under ladders.'

I had given up any immediate hope of a reconciliation with Lili's godfather when a letter came. His affection was heartening: 'I'm sorry if I used a sledgehammer but you're so single-minded I feel as if you're at the end of a long tunnel and I have to shout very loudly to reach you.'

Alison had begun working on a small farm while she considered other ways of financing a journey to the rain-forests. She often brought Lili a speckled egg or a jug of goat's milk and Lili sat on the floor chatting with Alison's philosophical feet.

Doran could now keep upright, or at least extend the business of falling over for three metres. Since his eyes were straighter and he could identify what he was doing he was better motivated by invitations out. Four metres of independent walking would be rewarded by a two-month holiday from his programme. One of Lili's favourite haunts for this activity was the home of a six-year-old boy called Jellal.

Doran knew his routine was to totter ten times into the dining-room, encouraged by bite-sized peanut-butter sandwiches, before he eventually sat down at the table. His sister counted and kept a firm hold on the sandwiches.

The children invented make-believe games which Lili acted out for us at home.

'But when you play with Jellal you don't always have to be a nurse or a princess,' I complained.

'The children at school say girls can't be doctors or knights or princes.'

She pursued this argument so inflexibly that, in desperation, Alison reached for a Ladybird reading book and plunged into a story without reference to the fact she had exchanged the children's names.

'No! No!' cried Lili.

'Yes! Yes!' shouted Alison. '*Jane* is going fishing and *John* is making tea.'

Eventually, when Lili had succeeded in wresting the book away from Alison, she looked thoughtful. 'It's true John does get all the fun. Why don't they really write it your way?'

'Lili spends a lot of time waiting on Doran. We should get him to do things for her,' Alison pressed.

Doran began his road to emancipation by passing Lili her night things, usually towed across the living-room floor in his teeth like a puppy. This was followed by a few exuberant attempts at cleaning her shoes which had to be terminated because he seemed to mistake the brown polish for chocolate sauce (previously unobtainable).

One day Lili arrived home from school quiet and crest-fallen. After a little encouragement she announced: 'I'm never going to paint again, they all say I'm messy.'

She didn't like keeping between the lines.

Lili's paintings were a kind of cosmic soup from which castles and angels appeared and disappeared by happy accident. Like Picasso she could say, 'I do not seek I find.'

I put my arms round her.

'Lili, they're wrong; painting is about discovering hidden things, it's magic. I'm a painter like you and I know.'

'My teacher won't understand . . .' She went over to the cupboard and took out her paints. ' . . . But I do, I'll make my kind of pictures at home and I'll do the tidy sort at school.'

The next occasion we were at Jellal's, Doran bit into his peanut butter sandwich and walked four metres from the kitchen to the living room. We were ecstatic.

Lili reached over, caught Doran's mask and put it upside down on her head.

Two months of freedom was hard to imagine.

'Try not to structure everything, Linda,' Peter advised over the phone. 'For heaven's sake, just do nothing for once.'

Applying this advice in a confined space with over-excited children who crave adventure and entertainment is not as easy as it seems. A more plausible solution was to sit round the table each week and make a seven-day plan so that everyone had something to look forward to.

During this period, to Lili's glee, Doran began getting 'into' things and proved he could be unashamedly naughty by refusing to get out of them.

Her own mischief was, as a general rule, fun, but her disarming habit of always telling the truth even when it was patently not in her interests to do so altered. Conversations like,

'I can't find any more raisins.'

'I ate them, Mummy.' Or

'The bathroom towel is very wet!'

'I was washing it, Mummy' were unexpectedly transformed by the response

'Doran did it.'

If anything was lost, broken or generally messed about there existed one irredeemable, but happy culprit. Lili ceased to admit to her own indiscretions. She told stories almost as unbelievable as her previous honesty.

I was mystified as to how such a pillar of truth could have been toppled. The next time I met her teacher I broached the subject.

'Lil's suddenly begun to tell lies. Can you explain it?'

'Yes, they all do, of course; isn't it wonderful she's beginning to be like the rest of her class.'

The term drew on and Lili made no noticeable advances in the areas of reading and writing. I had a lot of theories about education but limited experience. Nevertheless, I set out to design a stimulating educational programme which would inspire Lili to read. After four days in action the approach looked less rosy and the tenor of our exchanges corresponded more to those of a Victorian Dame school. I admitted ignominious defeat.

'Why won't you listen?'

'I don't want you to be a teacher.'

'Why not?'

'You did that all day with Doran. You ought to *play* with me.'

The honeymoon ended in April. We spent the last of it on the Isle of Wight so that Lili could continue her Easter holiday with my parents while Doran and I went back to America. When we were reunited I discovered that with some knowledgeable intervention from her grannie she had begun to read.

No one minded that the honeymoon was over, even Lili found her untethered brother slightly overwhelming; the weather had suddenly improved and she could use the swing and the climbing frame again. Doran's goal was to reach eighty metres of non-stop walking so an outdoor life was going to be essential.

At the beginning of the new term Lili's carefully provided wholefood lunchbox began arriving home half-eaten and she had no appetite for tea.

'Don't you like what I make for you?'

'Can I have that other bread sometimes – the "white" kind?'

'They swop,' the teacher explained. 'Caroline has taken Lili under her wing.'

Caroline came home at my first invitation.

'Keep your cardigan on, Lili,' she said, 'or you'll catch cold. Shall I ask your mum to make you a hot drink?'

When it rained Caroline was included in the party that escorted Doran on his walking practice around the main terminal at Gatwick airport. Here her mothering took a more radical turn.

'Lili and I would like chips,' she said, as the smell of frying drifted over from the cafeteria.

Saturdays brought us back to Jellal who luckily lived on a housing estate alive with small boys and their infinite supplies of transportation. I plucked a black plastic sub-machine gun from a muddy pool by the gate.

'Grab this, darling, and there's an armoured car over there on the verge.' (I could forgo my pacifism in my eagerness to see her joining in.)

Doran walked steadily along the road and was towed back on somebody's saddle to begin again.

'Is that your brother, Lili?' they asked. 'What's wrong with him?'

'He's brain-injured.'

'Why doesn't he cry when he falls over? Why does he have to do all that walking?'

After her bedtime story Lili took my hand.

'Will they always want to know everything about Doran?'

'Only as long as he's obviously different.'

'I wish I was brain-injured.'

'They'd ask questions about you if you had green hair and a nose like a pig, but you're lovely the way you are. When they want to know why something is different, it doesn't mean it's better!'

'Doran does sound a bit like a pig,' she said, 'especially when he's eating spaghetti.'

Another trip to America was scheduled for the beginning of September, when, as had become the custom, Lili would stay on the Isle of Wight.

Doran came home with a programme that included walking up and down hills and across rough ground. Executing this throughout a cold wet English winter was not inviting; however, I fixed my mind on the goal ahead rather than the daily inconvenience of getting there.

Anticipating a loving reunion with Lili, I rang my mother to ask which Portsmouth train I should meet. I learned that Lili had started at St Wilfred's School in Ventnor, and they both wanted to continue the arrangement until half term.

For some time Doran looked eagerly for Lili whenever I came back from shopping. She sent postcards and talked on the phone.

'Grandpa and Grannie have a toilet upstairs, Doran, and they let me watch television. Can I speak to Mummy? Mummy, there's a little girl called Louise who's come to live next door. I can get to her house through a hole in the hedge and, Mummy, Grandpa puts sugar in my tea. Do you mind?'

After each American trip we had to begin fund-raising for the next. Lili had travelled to Ventnor clutching sponsorship forms for a sunflower that Bert was growing to the projected height of twelve feet. St Wilfred's enthusiastically pledged money.

'They do understand our family, Mummy,' Lili wrote, the sentiments hers, the guiding hand unmistakably Grannie's.

At half term she came, not to resettle herself, but to make a good case for staying in Ventnor until Christmas. Her grandparents were all her own, they had become the extra thing she needed.

Alison bore the news stoically. Having at last organized a departure to the tropical rainforests she had been relying on Lili's imaginative humour to distract her mind from malevolent presences likely to writhe amid the dark slime of the jungle floor.

Our new volunteer was on the verge of an emotional breakdown when she arrived. I was glad in many ways that Lili had found a warm secure place where reality was also composed of soft towels and talcum powder, and people who would give all their time to her.

Just after this, I phoned Theresa to ask if she and Peter would write to Lili. I explained where she was.

'My God, Linda, you've not sent her away?'

'No, I haven't.'

'You have, my girl. I mean that's the upshot of it. She's been pushed out by your obsession with Doran.'

'Please, Theresa.' The phone was not a happy instrument to continue our discussion. I listened to my friend berating me for a few more minutes and then since I could afford neither the cost of the call nor its emotional drain, I hung up.

'Why do you go on expecting understanding when you know you won't get it?' Alison demanded, hugging me. 'You look shattered.'

'There's no way back,' I said and, thinking of Lili, led Doran outside for his long march up and down the wet and windy slope from which the last blackberries had long since been stripped.

Lili came home in December. All the way from the station she was anxious to see Doran walk. I took them both out into the fields behind the cottage. Doran, carried away with pride in his sister's attention, surmounted a molehill, staggered down the other side and clutched Lili's hand to keep upright.

'Can I take him to school now?' she implored. 'The one I go to with Grannie?'

'Don't you want to be here for next term?'

'I do love you, but Grannie and Grandpa will miss me and I promised the cats I'd come back.' She paused. 'You don't mind, do you, Mummy?'

Thus Lili incorporated the two homes in one. Knowing she was happier having made the choice and that she was free to change her mind at any time increased my confidence in this new state of affairs. Another letter from Peter began: 'Theresa tells me you were in tears on the telephone, but perhaps, if not ideal, this is a better solution for Lili.'

When it was time to take Lili back to the Isle of Wight, I decided there was enough untapped rough terrain on the island to justify Doran's having a change of location for a few days.

Lili arrived home from her first day of the new term, 'Mummy, Miss Burke says you must both come into assembly tomorrow.'

Lili met us at the door, guided Doran up the hall and sat him at the front facing the children.

The headmistress spoke. 'All the sponsorship money is now collected for the sunflower,' she said, 'but first of all I want the whole school to see that Lili really does have a mummy. There she is, and she's brought Doran.' Everyone cheered.

' . . . He's a very lucky little boy to have such a brave elder sister . . . What hymn have you chosen for us to begin with, Lili?'

'Specially for Doran, "Morning has broken",' she said.

Alison left for the tropical rainforests later in the New Year. Even before this eventuality I had decided that since we no longer had patterners coming in regularly the programme needed two CSVs and when Lili arrived at half term I was apprehensive to see how she would reclaim her place in the house.

'How's Doran managing?' she asked in the car. 'How are the helpers? Is Doran still naughty? Are you painting again Mummy?'

Doran was having some of his mud removed after a march through wet rough terrain when Lili burst in.

'He shouldn't be sitting like that – he should be on his tummy. Doran, I'm going to keep your helpers in order. I've a present for you when you've done your brachiation, it's a matchbox car. Can I see my bedroom?' She dashed upstairs. Sarah who was now masking Doran while she put on his shoes, raised her eyebrows.

'Your sister's bossy,' she said.

'It's Lili's way of not being a stranger,' but I guessed Sarah would want a little more proof before she revised her judgement.

Lili reappeared to demand that Elvira make her a cup of hot apple juice while Sarah and I settled Doran into his jacket. She left the drink cooling and climbed up on the arm of the sofa to reach for the photograph album.

'I want to show you our daddy, Doran. Mummy, does Doran know what his daddy looked like?'

Lili turned the pages while Doran smiled and dribbled on the images of his sister's infancy. The past was always important to her. She jumped down and went to look in the kitchen.

'Where's Doran's high chair?'

'We only borrowed it from Diana. He doesn't need it any more so she took it back.'

'I liked it! Why didn't you wait to ask me, Mummy?'

Sarah pursed her lips and said, 'Lili, there's hardly any space in the kitchen as it is.'

We finished the patterning and the two children sat at the table and had tea together. Before the first pieces of toast had been crunched and their crumbs fallen to the floor, Lili had begun to sneeze. She would arrive in what appeared to all intents and purposes the picture of health but somehow she invariably caught a cold. Judith told us colds were symptomatic of partings; my mother said it was the damp in Marsh Green and herbal remedies instead of Strepsils and Benylin.

All the ladders had gone except one which was now fixed a foot higher so that Doran could learn to swing like a monkey. This would help to increase his chest size and improve his respiration. It looked fun to Lili who climbed up and swung herself nearly half way along. Elvira caught her as she let go.

'Bravo, do it again, you are very strong.'

'I have to be to look after Mummy and Doran.'

Lili summoned Elvira to kiss her goodnight. Ten minutes later a small face appeared from the stairs.

'Can I have Sarah too, please.'

Next day when Sarah was showing Doran how to cook biscuits she found Lili at her elbow.

'Please can I help?'

'Yes, of course. Will you find the coconut, it's in the cupboard.'

While munching the results round the table at tea time, Lili pulled my sleeve,

'Mummy,' she announced, 'I've settled in.'

Sarah was staying until November but Elvira went back to Germany just before the summer holidays. She wrote to tell Lili who phoned up to say goodbye. I tried to soften the parting.

'There's a boy called Neil coming, he sounds lovely.'

'It won't be the same. There's nobody like Elvira.'

CSV wrote that Neil was a talented athlete for whose survival an early morning run followed by a gargantuan breakfast were absolute necessities.

While I was worrying about how I would afford the food bills Lili said, 'I think we need a man. A man makes a family.'

Fortunately, Neil's breakfast turned out to be no more than two bowls of cornflakes. When Lili came home she was always down early to demolish her poached egg at his side and practise her own warming-up exercises. Quite soon, and generally before Neil was out of earshot, she began asking: 'Do you love him, Mummy?'

'He's very kind.'

'All the other children at school have daddies. I'm the only one without one. Why don't you marry Neil?'

'Lili, you'll frighten him away if you say things like that.'

In August Sarah had a holiday and Neil and I took Lili, Doran and his programme to the Isle of Wight.

'It sounds like a rest,' I said as we spread our chaos into the train, 'but we have to work twice as hard to achieve half as much as at home.'

Lili said, 'I'm going to give you some fun, Mummy, too much work is bad for you.'

Entertainment started sometime before 6 a.m., when my bedclothes were removed.

'Come on, Mummy, let's go to the playroom.'

Doran scrambled along the corridor after her, and I dragged the eiderdown behind me. Neil found us there at 7.30. He brought me a cup of tea and escorted the children downstairs. The next morning he relieved me of this prematurely generous holiday atmosphere and sent me back to bed. Lili approved of the change because she liked Neil and I was much more fun if I wasn't yawning all day.

We had daily picnics with my parents on the beach. Neil and I took the respiratory jacket and the metronome and proceeded good-humouredly with the curious spectacle of patterning Doran while Lili dug a trench in front of him and filled it with water. She brought shells and a pile of sand so that he could build his own castle.

'Mummy, when will Doran be like other children? Does he always have to lie there when everyone else is in the sea.'

'Do you want a paddle?'

'It's lonely by myself.'

My mother appeared with wet seaweed and a fossil collection.

'I've found some children for you, Lili, they're behind the next breakwater, come on.'

Neil was very tanned, I noticed how his brown eyes sparkled. Doran was busy with his shells and for a moment I was fooling about, at least verbally, with a young man in the sunshine as if I had nothing particular to do with my time. Later Neil took Doran on his rough terrain so that Lili and I could escape to the children's zoo. This was largely equipped with empty cages, unless you counted the sparrows for whom bars were no barrier.

' . . . So perhaps there were big blue mice in these cages.'

'Or huge green rabbits, Mummy. When will you marry Neil?' she said.

On the way home we stopped at a little fair on the beach. It was so hot I ran into the sea and swam in my clothes. Neil dissuaded Lili from joining in.

'Mummy will have to walk home. She's too wet to sit by me,' he said but he made room in the back of the car all the same.

Before the summer had passed, Alison came back from the rainforest with a new philosophy of life. She began to credit things that can't be measured and in September she enrolled as an acupuncture student at a college of oriental medicine which, coincidentally, happened to be in the nearest town.

'Does Alison have a boyfriend?' Lili asked when she next arrived.

'No.'

'Then she'll have no one to marry.'

'Why do you want people to marry so much?'

'Everyone needs a family,' she said. 'We haven't got a

complete family without a father. I wish you'd understand, Mummy. Doran needs a father.'

The next trip to America provided us with a mechanical respirator in which Doran was cheerfully incarcerated for eight hours a day. He also became the proud owner of ski boots and ski shoes which were worn to encourage slow, straight walking since it is very difficult to run or cross one's legs in ski shoes without falling over. He had to walk on dry carpet. The answer was to erect a forty-metre long polythene tunnel in the garden. This swallowed it up but allowed Doran to proceed in not such cold comfort during the winter snows.

As they grew older, Lili and Doran formed a union. As soon as she came home she would hide him with cushions – 'It's all right, Doran, they won't get you' – or, at the first opportunity, pull him after her into the bathroom and bolt the door.

'Let Doran out and you can cook tea. He can help from his respirator,' I bargained.

At that time Doran's respirator forced him to lie on his back on a mattress on the floor. If he screwed his neck round far enough he could watch Lili stirring her ingredients into a large mixing bowl by his side and wait hopefully for an invitation to lick the spoon.

Sometimes this approach worked. When it didn't she might storm upstairs saying, 'Doran and I can never do anything together.'

'You do.'

'Yes, but it's always your way,' which was true. Everything had a time limit on it. We couldn't simply exist. We lived under pressure, and the older Lili grew, the more conscious she became of it.

'Exactly why is Doran like this, Mummy? I want to know,' she asked.

I explained carefully about his blood group being incompatible with mine.

'Why wasn't I brain-injured too?'

'Because you were my first child, Lili. The problem didn't affect you.'

Lili remembered all this carefully and told it to her best friend in school.

Just before she came home for half term my mother phoned.

'Lili's had a difficult time over the last weeks. A girl in her class discussed the problem of incompatible blood groups with her parents. She was told that Lili's birth caused the antibodies to form in your blood and that they produced the jaundice which was responsible for Doran's condition. Naturally she reported back and now all the children are telling Lili that she caused Doran's brain damage. Of course I've told her it's not true but she's sensitive and the words affected her deeply.'

When we met I was struck by Lili's unhappy clouded face.

'Tell Doran I'm sorry, Mummy.'

'What for, my darling.'

'Because it's my fault he is like he is, I was first.'

'Darling, it's nothing to do with you, it's biology.'

'I can't face Doran.'

'Lili, you are not to blame for Doran's injury, far from it. It's because of you that he's surviving so well and he's going to get much much better.'

'But Mummy, he's suffered and he can't run about and play like other children, and I can.' Tears streamed down her face.

'Lili, that's Doran's journey, not yours. It seems hard to you but you've given up a lot of your life for him. You're both brave.'

'It doesn't seem like I'm brave' she said.

CHAPTER 6

Lili Faces Herself

'Do you still worry about Lili?' Alison asked. 'Doran's going to be demanding for a long time yet, and you're under constant strain. Will she stay with your parents for ever?'

I winced because it was Christmas Eve and I'd banished all the hard questions. Lili had been a visitor at home for a year and three months.

'No, Alison, she'll come back sooner than you think. As yet she never asks to stay.'

'She's afraid you'll say "No". You're burying your head in the sand.'

Lili and Neil came back with bunches of holly. 'Star light, star bright, I wish I were I wish I might have the wish I wish tonight,' Lili chanted, as she jumped back and forth over Doran. He was now confined on his stomach with his arms and legs projecting out of the respirator cage with its vivid blue cover; he looked like a large turtle.

Then she stopped.

'Is it true Neil won't be here next time I come? He should *marry* you, Mummy.'

'Neil is twenty-two and I am thirty-eight, Lili.'

'You said age wasn't important,' she protested.

'It isn't Lili, in heaven,' I replied.

'Mummeee, you can't wait to go there!'

After Easter we put the respirator in the cottage extension

99

and opened the french windows so that Doran was almost outside. He endured the machine for eight hours a day. Although he was a courageous prisoner he asked continually for his sister and rejoiced whenever she returned. I watched my daughter's enthusiasm. She was still young enough not to be over-critical of the kind of life she had to lead. I saw no hope of establishing a superficially conventional family by the acquisition of a husband. Neil was already part of the wider family our eccentric progress had collected. The affection Lili intuited belonged to her ideal world, and in her wisdom she was able to see the difference.

Our summer volunteers, Dave and Amanda, showed a strong rapport with both children. Dave, a poet and a natural surrealist, invented the ingenious Mr Plumpton who committed continual outrages, such as replacing Lili's breakfast with a pair of slippers.

No matter how often Lili or Dave consigned him to the grave, Plumpton rose resplendent from his own ashes to reinstate himself in their conversation.

'So, the princess married a frog, Lili.'

'She didn't, she married Plumpton.'

I was curious that a child with such a delightful imagination should be so uninterested in silent reading. My mother had said, 'She's like you. You preferred being read to.' Lili's school report laid emphasis on the expression with which she read aloud. These thoughts comforted me but the contrast between the clear way in which I was tackling Doran's problems and the confusion of even identifying Lili's niggled.

Doran's early morning run was now half a mile round the recreation ground; this Lili was not anxious to share despite his demands that it was her duty to do so. Amanda hadn't been with us long before her excursions out, accompanied by Doran and the stopwatch, always included Lili.

One day Lili asked, 'Can Lord Winterbourne come to tea?'
I looked incredulous.

'It's true, Mummy, Amanda met him on the rec and now he plays with me when Doran does his running. Amanda's sure he's a real lord.'

I made cucumber sandwiches and regretted that I had no Earl Grey tea to offer. Lili's young aristocrat swept in on his bicycle. At closer sight along the garden path he was perhaps twelve years old and on the tattered side.

'I could get you a bike, Lili,' he was saying as they came in. 'Jes 'ave to talk to me Dad about it.'

'Mummy, this is Lord Winterbourne.'

'Lloyd, Lili,' he corrected her. 'Lloyd. Do any of you smoke?'

'Have a cucumber sandwich, Lloyd,' I said.

'No fanks, I eat at home.'

He winked at Doran who was once more incarcerated in his respirator.

All that summer Lloyd appeared and disappeared without invitation. He seemed to own an infinitely varied collection of new things which he brought once to be admired and never referred to again. Above all he was painstakingly nice to Lili. She treated him with charming gentility. Her old acquaintances did not call to see her. We were out of the way and she had made no strong connections when she went to the local school.

Lili was less insistent that I should marry Dave because she wanted him for herself, although there was always the question of Plumpton.

'He could be best man, Lili?' Dave suggested.

'No, he'd be worst man.'

'Plumpton wouldn't like that.'

'I'm not having Plumpton at my wedding.'

It was at this time that I noticed a change in myself. I was unaccountably more fatigued. The sheer physical exertion of performing most activities had begun to turn them into duties. I felt heavily reliant upon Amanda and Dave to keep things going. Lili began hearing the continuous explanation for my not joining in, 'Mummy's tired.' She transferred her demands without rancour but not without reflection.

'Mummy, will you stop being tired when Doran stops being brain-injured?'

I tried sleeping for an hour during the day but when I woke my muscles continued to feel like water. I was ever hopeful.

'Lili, this will pass and I'll be better quite soon perhaps.'

I hadn't allowed for my own ill health in any of my calculations. I was meant to bounce back.

'Grannie will look after you.'

'Doesn't she have her hands full with you and Grandpa?'

'I'm no trouble, I'd help.'

But I needed to take Doran to America in September when Lili's autumn term began at school.

The book I had been writing about Doran was finished and full of very plausible optimism, but what could restore my vitality?

When we came back from Philadelphia the new regime was that he should have the benefit of the respiratory machine throughout the night. In consequence a third volunteer had to be found to monitor its pressure while he slept. Lili's room was thus occupied. Any immediate plans for her return would have to be postponed. My mother now seemed more active and healthy than myself.

Doing an intelligence programme with Doran or supervising the small amount of physical programme he had left was easy compared with being recognizably my whole self for the daughter who'd lived so long on the nourishment of her early security. At half term she told me: 'Some children love their mummies best, don't they, but I love Grannie and Grandpa best too. Is that all right?'

I nodded. 'The more people you can love the luckier you are.'

Doran's bed became a mattress on the living-room floor and his nightly needs ceased to be my responsibility. This meant that aside from the loud sound of the machine hissing and puffing I had the first opportunity of undisturbed sleep for six years. It helped, I perked up noticeably, but Doran was very bored, he needed a highlight to his week. Fate remained on his side – I tried the door of a small private school and found that the headmistress had once been one of my patterners. 'We want an art teacher,' she said. 'Do you need some help for Doran?' Thus I was enrolled as an art teacher and Doran as a pupil once a week on Thursday afternoons.

These expeditions into more commonplace experience provided him with a very unusual friend. I explained all about Kevin to Lili when I collected her from the station.

'When I first took him home he said he'd walk over my car.'

'Was he joking?'

'No, he started at the back and walked over the roof and down the bonnet. He's a sort of elf. His mother is widowed and poor like us. He's kind-hearted and extremely intelligent but at the mercy of energy he can't control.'

When Lili came in, Kevin was on the floor playing matching pairs with Doran. He took a frog-like leap onto the sofa and pulled a rug over his head.

'Oooh I'm scared and I'm not coming out.' He kicked his legs in the air and scattered cushions.

'You look like a great big beetle on its back,' Lili exclaimed.

'No, a squashed tomato,' he answered. 'It's a squashed tomato day today, everything is squashed tomato.'

'What would you like for tea?'

'Squashed tomato.'

'Doran and I are having scrambled egg. Mummy, give Kevin a squashed tomato.'

I brought Kevin and his mother over for the latter half of Christmas Day.

'What did you have for lunch, Kevin?' Lili asked. 'Squashed tomato or turkey?'

'*Sausage* and mash,' he said. 'Lovely.'

All three children had been hurt and were brave in their different ways, besides which they instinctively cared for each other.

On Boxing Day Lili dived onto my bed. 'I can't wait to see Kevin again, he's a sort of brother. Would Doran be like Kevin if he wasn't brain-injured?'

Kevin came almost every day. Watching him next to Lili gave me pleasure but I was also confronted by the contrast between his reading, writing and general co-ordination and Lili's own. With a sudden effort of realization I began to add up her problems.

'Lili, do you read and write as well as the other children?'

'No, Mummy.'

'When there's a race, do you usually come last?'

She nodded. 'It's horrid, they laugh.'

'Can you ride a bicycle? Do you catch a ball well with one hand?'

'No.'

'Is it possible that a little creeping, crawling and running would help?'

'Do you think I'm brain-injured?' she said brightly. 'I'd often thought I was but you were so busy with Doran and

I didn't want to be *another* problem.' Lili folded her arms and looked severe. 'You don't always have your mind on me, Mummy, so I can't tell you everything.'

In preparation, Alison and I took Lili to Tunbridge Wells and brought her a royal blue track suit and running shoes. She began doing warming-up exercises in the shop.

About this time Doran had commenced a second holiday from his therapy.

Alison was dubious. 'You're taking one child off the programme and putting another one on it. Poor Lili.'

I had become convinced that thousands of children with very minor problems could be freed from them. I was also sure that the root of much emotional and psychological suffering lay in refusing to diagnose the difficulty as neurological. It was the treatment that mattered, all families needed to know where to find it ... Lili was not an enthusiastic crawler but she wanted to be as sporty as her peers.

'If you read to me, Mummy,' she said, 'I wouldn't notice I *was* crawling.'

So I delivered countless stories which Lili learned by heart and repeated back to Doran while he ate his tea.

Running along the well-beaten track to and from the nearby bridge was difficult. I was now asking Lili to master a rate I could hardly manage myself. A better plan was to take her over to my parents and establish a route along the promenade. I could then watch her, while she fixed her eyes on the pier amusements growing enticingly nearer.

Judith and Michael returned to England during Lili's next half term. They found her crawling round Doran's respirator in a figure of eight between the kitchen and the living room.

'Would you like to come to Vermont for the summer and do a programme with us?' Judith suggested. 'Michael and

I go jogging, and with the university so near we could even drum up some patterners.'

After a pause Lili answered, 'No, thank you, I want to be with Mummy and Doran.'

'If you change your mind the offer's open.'

'Please don't talk about my exercises, it's boring. Mummy, come and wash my back in the bath.'

When the door was safely closed behind us she whispered through the steam, 'If I go to Judith's do I have to do a programme?'

'Not if you can stick at it until the Easter holidays.'

By the end of term Lili was eight and a half. Her true grit had run like sand through the hourglass but the holiday had been won. Lili was a better reader, more co-ordinated and much more active but very out of temper with the floor. What might have happened if we'd done more or with greater intensity remained elusive.

Before Easter, Doran had joined his sister on the Isle of Wight. We took with us an understanding CSV, a psychology graduate called Tracey. It was early April and the leaves were still knotted into buds on the trees, but the sky was blue and the sea sparkled. Doran had gained one usually unremarkable attribute. He could stand still. For the first time in his life he wasn't dependent on having some thing or someone to hang on to. Lili decided we could take him to the island's best adventure playground. Here Doran only cared that where she went, so too (with Tracey behind him) did he. I held my breath till it hurt.

'Make friends, make friends, never never break friends,' Lili sang as they crossed a rope bridge in single file.

'Mummy, do you ever break friends with people?' Lili called. 'Sherry keeps breaking friends with me.'

'Who's that?'

'She's in my class.'

'What about your other friends?'

'I don't have any at school.' She swung herself onto the walkway. 'Push Doran up please Tracey!'

'But you used to be so happy.'

'That was in Miss Qualow's. Now I'm in the top class. I'm not really like the other children, they don't understand me or Doran.'

'Are you unhappy at school?'

'No, Mummy. I *like* playing by myself, it gives me time to think. Can Doran slide down that pole?'

She saw that I was about to ask another question.

'Please, I don't want to talk about it any more today. Don't worry, I'm all right.'

I was already tired and had to walk slowly.

By the time we'd reached the turnstiles the doors were locked.

The walls were all high and impossible to climb. Doran cried. Lili made faces to console him. Then she told him not to be a baby. He bit her, she shook him. A fight was in progress when a huge red setter bounded on top of them. He bounded off when the caretaker appeared.

'I don't usually take Chips for a walk at this time,' he said. 'You lot are lucky you didn't have to wait until morning!'

The holiday had much to commend it but it provided no easy answers for Lili's immediate future. Lili had been living with her grandparents for two years. They adored her but she was lonely and isolated at school. She was bright and receptive but she wasn't coping as well with ordinary school work as her peers. Children were sometimes cruel to her, which she bore with her usual poignant stoicism. I knew that there had to be some change.

Her headmistress told me, 'The staff and I all feel that if there was one child we could choose to take home with us it would be Lili. She's a very deep little girl. We can look after her while she's here but she *is* different and she does get teased.'

Tracey, my mother, Lili, Doran and I spent a wet morning at the Sandown Jacussi. This was a small cubicle with a bubbling pool and seating for no more than six.

'Mummy, I'm drinking with my skin. Can I be bare? The attendant did say we could. She said there were no men booked in for half an hour.' Lili was already untying her halter neck. We had just wriggled out of our costumes when three haggard youths seeking respite from the effects of the previous evening's revels appeared in the doorway.

Lili shouted, 'If you don't mind, we're not wearing clothes! No men allowed.' And then by way of an apology, 'My brother has a penis but it's too small to count.'

They vanished.

Before I took Doran home we booked Lili a return ticket to Boston. She persuaded us that her stay with Judith and Michael in Vermont should last six weeks. There was no doubting she could hold her own on an aeroplane. To her, America seemed scarcely farther than the Isle of Wight.

She came home a week before the flight brimming with excitement. This period presented a perfect opportunity to go up to London for an afternoon with the Marinkers. On the train Lili read the headlines of other people's newspapers.

'Mrs Thatcher's not going to give any more money to British Airways,' she said. 'I don't think that's fair because they fly Doran now.'

She squeezed my hand, 'I'll be all right when I'm grown up, Mummy. You were, Grannie told me.'

As we sat in the spacious garden of their old London house, I wondered what Peter and Theresa made of us.

Lili put her head in my lap and tickled my nose with a long blade of grass. 'I love you, Mummy.'

'She looks very well,' Peter said, 'and you both seem happy.'

'You see,' I said, 'You have to give us time.'

He smiled dubiously and Lili ran off to find Daniel.

On the day of her departure Lili's case was packed and her passport safe in a wallet round her neck.

Doran, in the charge of his volunteers, waved goodbye at the gate. It was Lili's moment. Alison was driving. Before the last roundabout outside the airport we heard a thump underneath us, the car bounced to a halt and one of the brake shoes lay in the gutter. We were just far enough away to lose the flight.

'Stop someone, Mummy,' Lili suggested calmly.

I stood by the roadside poised to beg a lift from the first vehicle I saw. It was in fact a yellow Gatwick van into which Lili, unflustered and optimistic, climbed, towing her own suitcase which was new and had wheels (and of which she was very proud).

'What flight is it?' our rescuer asked.

I was stupefyingly dumb.

'Virgin Atlantic, Mummy.'

We handed her over to an air hostess repeating our goodbyes.

'Don't worry,' she insisted happily. 'Look after Doran, I want to see him run.'

Over the summer we received long glowing letters from Judith accompanied by Lili's postcards which bore familiar marks of sweat and toil in their creation.

At home a BBC camera crew were now filming Doran's progress over a year for the documentary series *QED*. They were with us for two days the week before Lili came home.

Since my book on Doran had been published, the limelight had been on him. Lili held a great many opinions on the matter but to the media these were a side issue. It was the readers of *Doran* who made up for this neglect. She had been remembered in their letters. The pleasure she took in the exchange of drawings and postcards with Renée Forsythe, a lady from Scotland who wrote children's books, confirmed the view that a dram of real appreciation has great tonic value.

Lili reappeared on English soil looking taller and more of a tomboy.

'I missed you all and Grannie and Grandpa and the cats of course, but I imagined everybody was there with me. I even talked to you. Could you hear?'

Before she had been home a week she decided to complete her metamorphosis by having her hair cut short.

Kevin came round before she left.

'It's a "yes" day today,' he announced. 'In honour of Lili, Doran has to say "yes" all afternoon. Do you have any chocolates because I would like something nice to say "yes" to?'

'Kevin, will you come and stay with me on the Isle of Wight?' Lili asked.

'If my mother says "yes". Only it might not be a "yes" day for her. I hope it is though.'

I wished it were too, but I had to say, 'Lili, Kevin has to go to school next week. You'll see each other at half term.'

QED prepared to cover Lili's next homecoming. My mother had been briefed as to the exact train carriage they should travel in. The cameras were positioned on the platform in anticipation of a perfectly synchronized reunion. When the train arrived, seven minutes late, the door we faced swung open without disgorging Lili or my mother.

'Mummy!' Lili's voice hailed me from the opposite end of the platform.

'It split up,' my mother called, 'we're here.' We began

running towards each other in epic Hollywood style. *QED* bolted after us.

The BBC budget and the transient nature of the afternoon light made speed a priority. For this reason it was decided that our conversation would be recorded while we sat, like a line of dolls, along one of the station benches, which, as might have been foreseen, rendered us effectively dumb. Lili rescued everybody by climbing onto my knee. To the accompaniment of silent cheers she began, 'The boys in school are too bossy. I hope Doran isn't going to be like that.'

Then the camera crew fled home ahead of us to capture her meeting with Doran who was doing his sprints in the lane. This time they were on target. He flew straight past the finishing line and locked her firmly in his arms. She led him triumphantly towards the cottage singing, 'If you're happy and you know it and you really want to show it . . .'

Doran had lived on the Philadelphian programme for nearly six years. It was realistic now to believe he would one day go to a normal school and study and play football along with his peers. Despite his success, the Institutes were not yet happy to bless Doran's gradual assimilation into the classroom. Emotionally both children were well stretched. They had followed a long and winding road. I agonized . . . there was an alternative . . .

I had been significantly impressed by the results of a small centre in England called the Kerland Foundation whose staff were now giving shorter programmes with quite remarkable success. For months I'd been referring those families who couldn't contemplate a journey to Philadelphia to the centre's base near Taunton. The day had come to follow my own advice.

Doran's first evaluation at Kerland was wise and for us liberating.

The three-hour physical programme left time for school. We were given a more efficient respirator and for the time being, at least, Doran continued to use it at night. I was nervous of changing our habits too quickly. Weekends were to be spent in the pursuit of pleasure.

The search for a school willing to integrate Doran realistically was turbulent. Kevin's school had closed. The state schools in the nearest villages insisted they were too full. A church school, which endeavoured to practise what it preached, offered half a day a month. The Rudolf Steiner School had recently changed its policy on integration and anyway wouldn't accept the CSV needed to help with Doran in the classroom.

A friend who had once been a patterner dropped by unexpectedly while I was expostulating upon this dilemma. He drew my attention to Greenfields, an unusual private school which had recently moved into the district. Their philosophy was the education of children as individuals. Classes were small and even in the same class, children would often be doing different things. They maintained that learning would always be pleasurable provided children understood the reasons behind everything they were asked to do and the words used. They saw each child as only competitive against her or himself. Doran was interviewed and welcomed there among his peer group in the lower juniors on a half-daily basis. The trust fund I had set up for him with the royalties from my book paid the fees.

Doran's new respirator released him from his cage on the floor. Instead he wore a small respiratory jacket attached to a fifteen-foot hose leading to the machine. He could walk about.

'I don't believe it,' Lili said over the telephone.

And being driven home in the car she was still saying, 'You mean Doran can actually sit down at the table and draw with me and still be in his respirator?'

'Yes, and what's more he doesn't need to sleep in his respirator over Christmas.'

'Then can we share the same room and open our presents together?'

'Yes.'

She hugged my neck. 'Mummy, it's a miracle.'

We knew that after Christmas my mother expected to go into hospital to have gallstones removed. Lili couldn't sleep. It was not the excitement of Santa Claus that kept her awake. As I sat stroking her forehead she said, 'We lost Daddy and Great-Aunt Mabel. People do die. How do you know that Grannie will be all right?'

The best means of diverting her fear lay with Doran.

During his four-day holiday it was she who got him downstairs and produced their breakfast. When the adults appeared on Boxing Day, surprised but grateful for their extra sleep, they found the children jubilantly consuming a soufflé of brown rice, Christmas pudding and roast potato.

Just before the New Year we had a surprising letter. The National Bus Company presented awards to brave kids and Lili had been chosen as a 'Child of Achievement' for the work she had done on behalf of Doran. The ceremony, which included about a hundred other children from all parts of England, would take place at the Guildhall in London at half term.

I was wildly excited on her behalf.

Lili shook her head. 'They've made a mistake. I'm not handicapped – it must be for Doran.'

'Lili, what you've done is considered heroic.'

'But you did the work, and the helpers.'

For the next few days, my CSVs, Deborah, Andrew and Caroline, convinced Lili that the award would not be taken back when they found she wasn't Doran or an 'official' helper.

When the auspicious day arrived, Lili sat reflectively through two hours of presentations before receiving her medal.

'Aren't you going to wear it?' I asked as she stuffed it firmly back into its mock velvet box.

'It's too heavy, none of the other children are.'

We struggled to our feet in an attempt to shake off cramp but were immediately pressed back by rows of waitresses bearing plates of cakes, sandwiches and packets of crisps. Our final struggle to the toilet was waged through a close-packed flotsam of clowns distributing bags of sweets and party hats.

Lili began collecting things – 'For Doran and the helpers.'

A towering slice of Weetabix waving a microphone in its hand but with no apparent mouth, put his arm round her and invited her to sing.

'I don't know where its voice is coming from,' she whispered. 'Besides, it might laugh at my singing, the children at school do.'

Just then there was a call over the loudspeaker: 'Will Lili Scotson come down to the front row, please, Radio Brighton wishes to interview her.'

'I'm teaching my brother to play chess,' she told them, 'only he doesn't think it's fun unless he can take pieces and he moves pawns backwards as if they were queens.'

I was pleased to have been a reasonable companion on our expedition. The battery of extra vitamins I had been swallowing to remedy deficiencies shown up by a hair analysis seemed responsible for this improvement. I longed to believe they would slowly restore me to full health . . .

On the way across the square Lili began skipping.

'I'm really looking forward to Doran's face when he sees what's in this bag,' she said. 'You will let him have some of it, won't you, even though it is sweets?'

She skipped a little faster to catch me up and fell full length on the pavement, the bag flattened underneath her. Her tights were tattered and both her knees were grazed. The initial howl of pain faded into a more devastating realization.

'The chocolate's all squashed. Mummy, I'll have nothing to give to anyone now.'

'I have another bag. Look, it was a surprise, they gave it to me on the way out.'

We were sitting on the ground together in the February sunshine oblivious of the cold paving stones. As I cleaned up Lili's knees with spit and paper tissue, she said, 'Doran might think the chocolate was bought flat because he never has it and I can give the other bag to the helpers. Mummy, it's my silly mind that makes me fall over.'

We continued the conversation on the way home.

'I keep worrying about things,' she said. 'How to make Doran and you well and how to earn some money for us so that you can have a house near Grannie and Grandpa.'

I knew then that the long separation was almost over.

'Lili, do you want to come home in September?'

'I think so.'

'Would you like to go to Greenfields? It's a good school because they don't expect everyone to be the same.'

'Doran likes it there, doesn't he, so I'm sure I should. It's time I was a proper sister to him.'

'I thought you were.'

'I mean really teach him things, you know, games and stuff, he didn't have time before.'

At the end of the week *QED* arrived at the school to film Doran running an eleven-minute mile up and down the drive with his classmates pacing him and the rest of the establishment cheering them on. Lili followed part of the way and then vanished. I found her afterwards with

Caroline, her shoulders hunched up, near to tears.

'Mummy, I can't run like the others. Anyway, all they want is Doran. Doran's their hero.'

But the hero's moment of glory was already over; he was suffering extreme anti-climax, further exacerbated by the fact that I was detained by the producer who needed to film me writing down the names of my volunteers. I gave Lili five pounds and suggested she take them all out to the pub for drinks and crisps.

'When I've finished I'll bring French bread and cheese and bananas and ice cream for lunch. It was team work, Lili, and we all won.'

The sight of her now less than triumphant brother made my argument more convincing. She brightened with importance.

'Do you want to come to the pub, Doran?' She waved the five pound note. 'I'll treat you.'

Kevin appeared in the evening. Somehow Lili's medal got sat on and the clasp holding it onto the ribbon broke. I put it in the box and decided its effect was more striking when thought of as a coin. Lili seemed unconcerned; she was engaged in a good-humoured fight with her guest. When she grew tired he remained inextinguishable, pummelling her more violently because there was no retaliation.

Doran, respirator jacket still huffing away, shouted, 'No, Kevin, bad!' Then dragging his friend off his sister he lay upon her and let a battery of blows rain on his own back.

'Gosh, Doran would die to save your life, Lili,' I cried.

That night, when the others had gone out for a drink, Lili and I were left alone. Her brother lay asleep on his mattress in the middle of the living-room floor. The duvet rose and sank in response to his respirator jacket like the quilt I had seen covering a mechanical waxwork of the Sleeping Beauty at Madame Tussaud's.

Lili stopped pulling on her pyjamas to look down

thoughtfully. 'He does love me a lot, doesn't he?' Her eyes moistened. 'I really think he would die for me. Oh Mummy, will he ever be like us?'

'I hope so, darling.'

'I can't wait until September. I want to come home. Please. I'll look after him always.'

She pressed her head against me and wept as if her heart would break, but it didn't. Instead she began to smile. 'I'm glad I can let out some of my feelings. They get stuck deep inside, Mummy, and I try and try to let them come but they won't always. They go round and round inside.'

'Lili, I'll phone Greenfields tomorrow and let them know you'll be there next term, and Lili, Doran can come off nights in the respirator. His breathing's much better, you can both sleep together in the same room. Grannie will buy you a bed.'

'One like Doran's with drawers in it?'

'Yes, and a table for your writing and hooks to hang up your clothes. Oh my lovely daughter, I'm so glad you're coming home.'

I remembered Auden's poem:

> Restored returned the lost one borne
> Through seas of shipwreck home at last
> And swear the live long day to part no more.

I had her back. I'd fallen in love with her when she had been my unborn baby. She was my teacher and I still had much more to learn.

I took Lili back to Ventnor for the remainder of the term. My mother had been discharged early because she was healing so quickly and there was pressure on accommodation. I'd hoped that she would have company her own age in the hospital, although because of her youthful aura,

I was thinking of people of twenty-three, not seventy-three.

Lili was asked to bring her medal to school and explain how she came to deserve it.

'Did they understand?' I asked.

'Yes, but at break Sherry said: "Pooh, I got a better one than that for swimming." Don't tell my teacher, it only makes her unhappy and she can't do anything. Stop looking sad, Mummy.'

Lili arrived home just before Easter. Her old friends Andrew and Caroline had already gone. After the initial euphoria of a welcome for her and a leaving party for Deborah and Donna, my departing volunteers, whose absences she felt acutely, Lili seemed to drift in on herself. CSV had only managed to find us one volunteer, Louise, who was a non-driver. We both worked hard but I was plagued again by nausea and dizziness. Every movement was a sickening physical effort. Alison, studying for her finals, and in a tetchy mood, found little right with the world and children in particular. By July she too would be away. Lili felt both regretful at the prospect of losing a beloved friend and miserable that she could do little right. She retreated into her pile of tapes and curled up for what seemed like hours, headphones glued on, listening to the familiar and constant world of her stories. She cried easily and could not be prised from a state of physical inertia. When I sat beside her she would only say: 'I can't get Grandpa and Grannie out of my mind. I know they miss me. Mummy, are you ever going to get well?'

I had now ceased almost entirely to worry about Doran. My sleepless nights were spent over Lili. The promised future appeared to have become a nightmare. I felt increasingly sicker and could find no explanation from my consultant although steroids had now been suggested. I was on the verge of believing I was going to die before I could reach

118

Lili, and the image of my daughter having to endure the death of her mother was unbearable.

One Sunday Alison treated herself to a copy of the *Observer* instead of revising. She read out an article on a parasitic yeast called Candida which could proliferate wildly in a person under stress, causing chronic debilitating symptoms.

'It's you,' she said. 'Get the book *Candida Albicans*. I'll go and buy it for you.'

This was to be rescue at the eleventh hour. Within a few days I'd found my way to the remarkable Coburn Centre for Wholistic Cleansing in nearby Ashhurst Wood, where my wretched condition was diagnosed. With colonic irrigation, homeopathic preparations, superdopholus and a yeast-free diet, my gut, my liver and therefore my whole constitution slowly detoxified. Every time I came home from a treatment I looked less yellow.

I could sense Lili watching me waiting to find out how real this change was. When old ladies with sticks were no longer racing me in the streets I began to believe in my recovery.

At last Lili took off her headphones.

'You're young again,' she said.

I put out my hand. 'Come on let's go for a walk in the fields. We're going to start living in the here and now both of us. No more tapes.'

'Mummy.'

'No, I'm serious. Hit me if you like, be angry if it helps.'

'I can't.'

'Think of something I've done that made you angry.'

We climbed the stile and Lili sat down on a fallen log and looked at me with a new seriousness.

'When I first came back we went shopping and everyone asked about Doran, they didn't notice me. You should have told them who I was. Don't they know he has a sister?' Her cheeks flushed. 'I thought you'd be unhappy if I was angry. I've been trying to look after you.'

'Now you must be as cross as you like with me and with Doran.'

'Won't you mind?'

'Doran needs you to knock him into shape.' – Lili suddenly grinned.

'He does, doesn't he?' she said.

'And Lili,' my mind was racing, 'What about a holiday, just you and I?'

'A painting holiday!' she said 'Only we've no money.'

But money came from the Rowntree Trust who help families with special needs. Doran was carried off for a week by my cousin Polly and Lilli and I took a flat at Carbis Bay near St Ives. I deplored the wall paper. 'It will look all right tomorrow,' Lili said as she speedily covered it with pictures reminiscent of the best abstracts of the New York school.

When CSV sent David Westwell and Andy O'Brien, neither Lili nor I looked like the invalids of the previous month. The children's insults flew cheerfully across the breakfast table as Doran copied Lili's speech.

'Doran, shut up, you're boring,' Lili shouted.

'Shut up, you-are-boring, Lili,' answered her brother.

My renewed energies had spurred me to discover a consultant willing to provide Doran with powerful behind-the-ear hearing aids. This boosted his hearing to normal levels.

Lili reported developments.

'Boys can't actually marry their sisters can they? Because Doran's just said "I love you" and pinched my bottom. It's all right,' she said, 'he isn't a problem. He's a younger brother, and he's bound to be a pain at times but he's my very good friend too.'

CHAPTER 7

Sister and Brother

Individuals who are forced by circumstances to make unusual choices for their children must prepare to be talked
about. The motives behind criticism differ. I had to pick my
way thoughtfully and with an exterior of blithe unconcern.

The moment Doran's brain injury was diagnosed I lost
my independence. I found myself lectured by professionals
whose views differed from my instincts. All my physical
and mental energies were consumed by my children. I
wished for no other identity. I didn't want to talk about
what I had been or might be again. Anyone who would
help me, any kindness at all, however small (the smile of a
passerby), was a gift to me. I learned that the presence of
a child with severe chronic injuries makes people uneasy.
It cuts across the social contract which rests upon the
assumption that by bettering oneself materially one can
always get on in the world. Help is easier to give if one can
foresee a solution. I knew that acquaintance with gross
disability in a child introduces impossibly difficult questions. Time is no healer. It won't be resolved like a love
affair or a death. The state of crisis is permanent. The
anguish becomes worse as the child grows bigger and the
disability more evident. My claim that it could be overcome
only added further embarrassment. There were conventions
even to having a handicapped child. If you broke these,

many doctors, health visitors and physios, even some charities, felt betrayed.

From the beginning I wanted to enfold both children.
Whatever else, they would not have to suffer loneliness. No
reasonable advice to the contrary could keep them from
sharing my bed. Despite little sleep, I drew strength from our
intimacy, which was just as well because alternative sources
were in short supply. I had minimal opportunity to reflect
on how inadequate the state was at meeting any of the real
demands made by the birth of a child with severe long-term
problems. There were no provisions for Lili. One or both
children could have been taken into care, which seemed a
most damaging answer. My request for a few hours a week
of home help when we came out of hospital was refused.

The parting from Lili at Guy's became an act of faith. Once
more I seemed to be sacrificing my well, whole daughter for
my blind, deaf, screaming son. I never much liked the story
of Abraham and Isaac. The idea of guardian angels seemed
more attractive. I saw that if all three of us were unburdened
by selfish interests (because Doran's determination to go
through with all the pain and terror and live can hardly be
called selfish) then whatever happened we were already safe.

Once home, Lili's increasingly active relationship with
Doran became the key to our unity.

As we began the Philadelphian programme, less and less
people gave me advice about my son; I had found so many
answers. Instead, its effect on Lili emerged as the focus of
attention. I had objective arguments to justify my actions
in response to Doran's need. How Lili would grow up with
the experience was then debatable. I learned that regardless
of what people thought of me, if they could offer something
good for her I should be alert to it. This tendency to
look for what was positive in any situation freed me from
agonizing over people's motives. When Peter Marinker

became Lili's godfather, I knew that I should be hurt, but his real care and concern for her transcended all my discomfort. He saw me as a fanatic, and, sadly, protest against that accusation would be to conform to it. A fanatic is blinkered, whereas I could see painfully well in all directions. It was because of this that I daily blessed the route I had taken. The alternatives were starkly unbearable.

I longed for approval. It was hard at first to understand that many old friends who respected my painting found this present behaviour incredible. How could I cheerfully renounce all social life for both myself and my charming daughter in favour of a gruelling routine dedicated to a type of child who never prospered? Of the new friends I was discovering, few even mentioned the paintings which crammed the cottage. But they understood what I was doing and most of all why I was doing it. 'It's a gift to be simple, it's a gift to be free,' so the song goes, 'It's a gift to come down where you want to be.' Being simple had once been hard for me. Now I knew where to find simplicity in the midst of a seemingly unreasonable tangle of complications.

Sometimes I imagined Lili's jubilation should the house next door be miraculously inundated with children who would adore her. More often I accepted that there were limits to the things I could change – but then these limits themselves might alter too . . .

I forget how often I was asked if Lili was jealous. It was almost easier to agree. I examined the concept very carefully; the meaning of a word depends so much on its context. The phrases we use often manufacture feelings. In classical terms, Lili didn't lie in bed plotting to murder her brother. This wasn't her difficulty. What she wanted was for other people to recognize who she was and that she had a separate and individual worth.

Since I was always ready to forgive myself, I had no trouble

forgiving others and believing that they in turn could ultimately forgive me. The kindness that came as my daily bread
was powerful and heartening. Even at my lowest I maintained
a gentle self-mockery which prevented any further descent. I
forgave my own sins of personal vanity. I wanted Lili to see
me still a young, pretty woman and to enjoy my appearance.
As Doran got better, I found myself looking in the mirror
again and sent out for a bottle of Henna. I didn't lose the
impulse to climb trees or to swim naked in the deep pool at
the bend of the stream and put willow herb in my hair. I
still imagined I would dance all night and be first up in the
morning to dance again. Sometimes thoughts of falling in
love and having someone desire me were tempting.

As I became aware that I could not shake away the illness
which no one initially understood, I seemed to be reaching
out from my own dream to attend to the living things
around me. I understood the psyche of the chronic invalid.
Only the horror of the effect of any further decline roused
me. Untreated, Candida takes advantage of physical protests, making one a reluctant prisoner of slow motion.

I arrived at the Coburn Centre on my knees. Putting
myself into the hands of people who knew how ill I was
and who had the power to cure it was a singular heaven.
At that time I had gone to sleep night after night in terror
because each day the progress of the disease became more
marked and harder to bear. When the combination of
wholistic cleansing treatments caused the toxins to clear
gradually from my body and the nausea to subside I wondered how I'd borne it all so long.

My revival was the signal, a general renaissance of well-
being.

Lili's request to stay with my parents meant both dividing
our family and extending it. I'd watched grandmother and
grand-daughter, well aware that they had a naturally special

relationship. I knew my father thoroughly enjoyed children and took great pride in providing the role of Lili's best friend. Lili may have lacked speed and agility but her physical beauty and inner light gave her grace. She identified with the feminine side of my mother which concerned itself with insight and caring as well as good food and elegant clothes (selected with great ingenuity from the Oxfam shop).

When I felt anxious because I couldn't offer enough for my daughter I remembered in my own childhood being eager to spend long seaside holidays with my great-aunt because my mother was working. I was always proud of her and felt truly surprised when I discovered how much she'd worried about our separation. Children like an extended family, and Lili had appropriated her grandparents. Understanding this helped me to explain to increasing numbers of people where she was and why she hadn't come home. I was relieved to find support for the situation. Almost every step I took relied on the goodwill of other people for its success.

I was shielded and I was grateful. If gossip was relayed to me it was always thoroughly out of date.

My mother protected me over Lili. She had noted the things Lili unexpectedly couldn't do but refrained from adding them up and posting them to me. I knew my daughter had run very high temperatures. She had trouble reading, she dressed and undressed slowly . . .

Minor incapacities became invisible against a background of severe chronic disability. To misquote Oscar Wilde, 'To have one problem child is a misfortune, to admit to more is sheer carelessness.' Gradually I became aware that Lili's eccentricities wouldn't go away; she was eight years old and the issue had become serious.

Looking back it seemed that each time she had developed a furiously high fever there had been cumulative effects. Once she had undone buttons with tiny nimble fingers.

Before the measles she could certainly sing in tune. Again I was aware that there were no adequate tests available to help parents recognize minor neurological damage, because no early treatment officially existed.

Lili's IQ had been assessed at her school on the Isle of Wight. The tests that demanded the application of reading and writing were difficult for her and she scored low averages. On verbal reasoning her mark was high. However, the report indicated that this was probably due to the unusual verbal stimulation she received from her grandparents, an assumption prompting the psychologist to retain an overall mark of low average. If Lili's intelligence was low then either I had no conception of intelligence or the procedure of testing for it gave a very false picture of a child's capabilities. Fortunately, I found an ally in her head teacher who was also troubled by the injustice of the report.

I made up my mind that however much I was criticized, she should try a short daily programme. I knew I was afraid of what I would find.

Lili should have crawled reasonably well. In fact she seemed to have lost the idea entirely. This was interesting because I had watched her do it, albeit not early, for almost a year of her infancy. Since then she had contracted whooping cough, pneumonia and measles. I was also fairly sure that she'd managed some crawling in the early days of Doran's programme, before the measles. I aimed at least to increase her chances of establishing good cross-pattern co-ordination so that running with her arms swinging came naturally. This would give her the chance to close the gap between herself and her peers. The theory behind the programme was that cross-pattern movement encourages the growth of neural pathways. Creeping, crawling and running also develop respiration, both neurologically and physiologically. Once the neural pathways are forged they can be adapted by the appropriate stimulation. Up until this point Lili had fought shy of physical exertion by adopting a positive although considerably over-the-top feminine view of herself.

'Girls don't!' she would argue until she began to see that girls did and that she wanted to. She wouldn't wear jeans, she preferred verbal games requiring imagination not speed. She liked to paint. There was undoubted strength in her, although she purposefully restricted its scope so that she wouldn't fail.

Competing only against herself, she accepted a physical challenge. Her struggle was different from Doran's. She was wrestling with her image. She abandoned the pretty dresses for a track suit and the imaginary game for a real one. When she was reminded which hand and foot to move, a co-ordinated cross pattern emerged.

Lili needed to come home to find her perspective. Her philosophical personality combined with a poetical way of coping. To explain the disorder in which she most frequently found herself she invented a passenger dedicated to the frustration of nobler instincts.

'Why can't you put your clothes into a neat pile?'

'Mummy,' she would say, 'a voice in my head tells me not to do it. If I don't listen it gets cross.'

This voice was a little disconcerting. One evening when I tucked Lili up for the night I enquired casually about its character. Did it have a name, would it like a goodnight kiss?

'Mummy, are you mad?' she asked. 'I was just trying to explain to you what it feels like when I want to do something but I always forget and the more I want to the worse I am.'

Lili stopped talking about voices. I was too credulous. In the final analysis parents are obliged to be prosaic. The arrangement is that you support your children's flights of fancy whilst letting them know, without actually saying so, that your own feet are planted firmly on the ground.

Understanding why she felt different became a considerable asset to Lili. She had held in her frustration. She knew the world had built up a picture of her as the 'normal' child, which, compared with Doran, she was. She imagined that by revealing her own disabilities she would lose people's approval. She could only go on trying to be 'normal' and hoping she would wake up one morning to find out it was so.

Shortly after she had begun at Greenfields school I contacted the dyslexia centre in London. A different emphasis in the approach to IQ from the centre's educational psychologist shifted her from the bottom to the top end of the IQ scale.

'I think Lili needs to be reminded,' he wrote, 'that she is not a less able girl intellectually and that her verbal abilities are significantly high . . . this is quite consistent with your own report of her being a perceptive and sensible person, at times entering into quite deep conversation.'

The report was constructively valuable. Besides a school highly receptive to her needs, she gained another friend in her teacher for dyslexia, Mary Flecker, and a marked increase in her self-esteem. I realized the vital importance of distinguishing between a neurological problem arising out of physiological circumstances and a psychological problem. It is fashionable to attribute physical reactions to emotional causes, especially when a child's circumstances are unusual. I know too well, having lived for months with Candida undiagnosed, the tremendous and misleading psychological stress that wrong assumptions can cause. Treating the symptoms will only deepen the problem unless the source is also recognized and treated as a priority.

When Doran had been a year with the Kerland Foundation, Lili said, 'Doran's doing so well at his programme now, Mummy, I think he's a better reader than I am.'

'Are you asking for a programme again, Lili?'

'Yes. A really serious one. I didn't do *that* much at Grannie's. You see, Mummy, if Doran can read all those words that fast, I should too, shouldn't I?'

So Lili came with us to Doran's next evaluation. Margaret Baker, the clinic's director, assessed her carefully. The difficulty was remarkably straightforward. Lili was right-sided but her left eye was wholly dominant. This laterality problem had caused her troubles. Unlike a neurologically normal child who does most things automatically, Lili had to think consciously about her actions all the time in order not to make a mistake. She put more effort in for less return. There is a rhyme about a centipede who was happy until a toad in fun asked it which leg came after which. Once it was obliged to think about movement that had come naturally it was finished and lay distracted in a ditch considering how to run.

Lili had done better than that. She had tolerantly borne criticism from other kids for being slow and clumsy and from adults for not concentrating. Much of her dreaminess had been an escape from the frustration of having a body with a hidden flaw.

Her own programme consisted of wearing glasses with the left side covered, forcing the right eye into dominance. She was given activities which demanded the specific connection of her right eye with her right hand or foot – catching, bouncing and kicking a ball, skittles, tennis. We kept discovering more. This combined with brachiation, half an hour of creeping and half an hour of crawling, fifteen minutes of endurance running and ten eighty-metre sprints – all designed to mature her co-ordination and respiration. The programme meant she had to change her school hours and make up in the evenings what she missed in the mornings. I do not think anyone believed she would find the task easy. It wasn't a three-month programme, it was scheduled to last a full year and once she'd committed herself to it she had to work side by side with her brother.

Doran was delighted with the new regime. He flung himself into competition, shouting, 'I won' at every moment, having set the imaginary finishing lines himself. Gentle Lili refused to be beaten by a boy. Our volunteers at that time combined sheer *joie de vivre* with complete and serious dedication. These young women were both called Karen, although to make matters easier (or more complicated) one of them answered to the nickname Fred. They made life warm and dramatic, a party with a purpose. We were given shelter from the elements by the generosity of the manager of the East Grinstead Cannon Cinema, Sheila Chamberlain. Her kind-hearted staff cleaned round the children as they crept and crawled between the aisles and ran circuits through the auditorium.

After four months, Lili's writing was flowing along, with the letters all properly joined up. She had to be told to turn the light off at night and stop reading. She could run fast without falling over and she had started karate. By the time our new volunteers Louise and Tim took over she could bounce and catch a small ball. They looked amazed when I explained that she'd been unable to cope with a large one.

On the first day of spring she and Doran, intent on raising money for the Kerland Foundation, set off on a six-mile sponsored hike from our nearest village along the old railway to the cinema. Doran ran backwards and forwards most of the way. It was now undeniably easy for him to do something once thought impossible.

The real victory over disability was in fact Lili's. This was the longest she had ever walked in a day. The secret of her new ability lay with the change her programme had produced in her breathing.

Money was always crucial. Having a trust fund to take us to America did not mean we had enough to live on at home.

I remember that during the freezing winter of '78 the DHSS cold weather payments were deducted from my overall benefit. We were all just out of Guy's Hospital and snowed in. The Artists' Benevolent Fund then offered to pay the outstanding electricity bill but were not permitted to do so. This was my first taste of the inflexibility of the DHSS rules which do not allow claimants to receive charitable donations of money regardless of their potential to alleviate suffering. Every week we budget down to the last penny. It can be fun being perpetually like a student on a student's income, but a student is permitted to supplement her finances. She can see an end to her impecuniousness with the prospect of a well-paid career. Until that time she is responsible only for herself and her studies. I have already qualified by experience. This is my career, and my future as I see it will be to go on enabling Lili and Doran to enjoy their full personalities and physical independence and to help other families where possible. Lili wants me to paint but I can't. It's been so long. I can't play at it. Painting like playing an instrument needs the attention of your whole body. I can write because I can hold the pictures in my head and put them down on scraps of paper when I have time.

The amount parents like myself save the state is never officially reckoned. Many women and some men live on supplementary benefit because their commitment to the needs of their hurt child prevents full-time paid work. It seems only humane that they should be officially entitled to keep a little more of any extra income to spend on the specific urgent needs of their children or on their own health . . .

If I had submitted to fear of the range of possible disasters open to us I would have lost my emotional reserves overnight. I didn't need to cultivate an ability to detach myself. In times of crisis, instead of sinking I simply found myself standing back; I am perhaps still a painter after all.

I continue to survive on the kindness of other people. I realize too how much Lili has had to endure for being my daughter and Doran's sister, plus her own individual self with the complications of dyslexia and an artist's vision of the world thrown in. Surely half the books ever written are pleas for people to accept what is different in themselves and in others? Generosity of spirit always does reward the giver.

Last night Lili yawned and said, 'Having children is natural, isn't it, Mummy? Perhaps Doran will have them, he likes babies, but I don't want any. I'm going to be an engineer, but I'll still make pictures.' She snuggled down on her pillows, closed her eyes and went on, 'I'll do them for you Mummy because you had to stop.'

I pulled the window shut a little. The night air was cool and the aspens shook their leaves.

I have a kinship with the woods about our cottage. When I was nine I read a children's story in which a father's parting words to his daughter were: 'Remember life is an adventure.' The concept was fresh to me then and I thought it extremely wise and never to be forgotten. My life still is an adventure. I can only say, 'There we have been and by this route travelled.'

Doran is eight now and Lili ten. Both are slim and blue-eyed with light brown hair. Doran, despite his lack of overall co-ordination, is a meticulous orderer in his personal life. He hates to forget things and will get up in the night and beg Lili to go into the garden to retrieve a car he has left outside. He thrives on running and football and is forever transforming himself into a fast car or a motorbike. Before sleep he shouts, 'Goodnight, Lili, I love you. I'll be good tomorrow.' 'Just you do Doran' she says, throwing him his woolly elephant.

On Saturdays they both go riding. Lili won a painting competition at the stables for an expressive drawing of a horse. She has a reason for every line she uses. There are long stories behind her pictures, and joy and sorrow are closely mixed.

Doran rides like a cowboy crying 'Whoa' and 'Walk on!' every five seconds, turning his long-suffering mount in circles. Often they stay most of the morning at the stables. Doran carries buckets to the tap to water the horses. He asks endless questions. Lili answers him, I can't, I know nothing about horses.

When a stranger doesn't understand him clearly Lili says: 'My brother's still a bit brain-injured so you have to listen,' and Doran smiles.

'You are loopy, Lili,' he remarks.

'Thanks a lot, Doran. I only said you were brain-injured, not stupid! My brother's loopy, I forgot to say.'

'No, I'm not.'

'Yes, you are.'

'You are.'

'No, I'm not, you are.'

'No you!'

Lili is a comedienne, she can mime superbly. Doran has to be held down in the audience.

'My turn later,' he says as Lili attempts the splits sliding her feet out on two plastic bags.

'I think that's dangerous,' I say.

'It's not, Doran's doing it! Give him some more bags then he can be on hands and knees like a skating horse. It's a circus!'

At last they are both hauled off to their homework. Doran puts on his respiratory jacket while he does his. Lili sits down at the kitchen table and opens her books.

Lili created the atmosphere in which Doran could prosper. His independence is my gift to her; it is also her gift to him.

The connection between parents and children is a complex one. Like all love it is intended for mutual learning in order that we respond to the non-material forces which govern our lives as well as the material and the practical. I still make mistakes. I hope that I am never afraid to be wrong or to let Lili tell me over again that I must pick up the pieces and tread more carefully.

To be alive is always surprising and living is daily open to our questions.

TWO

The Other Children

CHAPTER 8

---•◆•---

When the Doctor Cannot Help Any More

Once upon a time there was a general feeling among people that having a brain-injured child would soon be a thing of the past. People didn't actually use the words brain injury because it was the external appearance of these children that affected them most. Even if they could walk and talk they looked odd. Not quite what you'd expect of a human being. But you couldn't really compare them to animals because if you did, animals, with all their alert instincts geared towards survival, came off best. So it was the vegetable kingdom that was looked to for analogy. The candidate whose form most closely resembled the human head was the nutritious but uninviting cabbage.

By the sixties women simply didn't expect to give birth to cabbages. There were all sorts of new tests to make sure your pregnancy was handled with the ultimate clinical sophistication. More hospital deliveries, better diet (they thought) and so on. The unfortunate cabbages who were born would either die very quickly or be evacuated to secluded institutions, although occasionally a neighbourhood might contain an oddity in a wheelchair sitting outside on sunny days. Normal children, of course, had

137

virtually no knowledge of what it could be like living with
a child who was different to the extent that the slang word
for him denied his humanity. Our village had its cabbage.
I remember him as they pushed him by. A kid older than
me but with a body half my size and a head that looked
twice as big. The thing was, he wore a grammar school cap,
a contradiction which remained puzzling.

Nothing new as a solution to the problem of brain injury
was researched in the big teaching hospitals. It was felt that
the situation would apparently take care of itself and the
handful of surviving affected children could be secluded,
for everyone's good, from the rest of the community in the
existing purpose-built institutions.

This is probably an over-simplification. It is also true.
The situation did not turn out as planned. Technology
could usefully save more infants than ever before. The
degree of possible developmental delay was hard to estimate
early. Rescuing a baby was humane. It was also prestigious
– the quality of such post-operative life was not the surgeon's concern. Nor was the problem confined to obstetrics.
Kids came out of major and minor operations with anaes-
thetic complications. The term meant that too much or
too little oxygen had probably been administered. The
elegant job that had been made of preserving life was off-
set by the words, 'I'm afraid your child will probably be
a vegetable.'

In England malnutrition is not now a primary cause of
injured brains but there are other causes: drugs taken during
pregnancy, food additives, crop spraying, lead in petrol.
The new chemical compounds developed to release people
from the domestic wheel were providing hitherto unim-
agined dangers, as were new levels of radioactivity.

Since a pregnant woman rarely asks for the statistical
chances of her baby having a problem, she does not question

what help will be available to herself and her family should the unthinkable happen.

Looking at *The Brain: A User's Manual* published in 1982 I see that 3.5 out of every 10,000 babies born have Down's Syndrome. If the mother is over forty the rate rises to 1 in 50. Spina bifida, often occurring with hydrocephalus, is present in 10 out of 10,000 live births. Mental subnormality, excluding Down's Syndrome, affects 17 out of every 10,000 babies. Two million Americans suffer epilepsy usually combined with other neurological disorders. Babies with athetoid cerebral palsy have injury to the motor areas of the brain. The symptoms include laboured respiration, involuntary writhing movements of limbs and face, and considerable speech difficulties. It can also cause visual and auditory problems which make public recognition of the sufferer's normal or even high intelligence an unlikely labour. Some children are simply blind, deaf or paralysed. There are many other labels for brain injury. Brain injury is regarded as too blunt a word. Infantile infections and inflammations can attack the brain. These can be the greatly feared viruses such as meningitis or encephalitis, or a virulent attack of the more common childhood diseases. Accidents, falls, electric shocks can also make a bright athletic child totally dependent upon the goodwill of the rest of us for the dignity of his survival. Many, many of these children would undoubtedly once have died. Before antibiotics, pneumonia eliminated a high percentage.

Medical technology has grown more sophisticated, increasing its power to save life. When your child's existence is not at risk, apart from routine medication which you may not want, his problems are considered social not medical. You're on your own.

Modern policy is to run down institutions and keep the child in the family. Families whose expectations have been high do not want to put a baby they already love or the child they have nurtured into a home. They do not understand why the doctors who have demonstrated much skill and innovation in other areas of medicine should be pessimistic on the subject of the brain, and they are not without hope that the diagnosis could be wrong. So the child with the injury which could be reflected in a multitude of different physical and mental symptoms goes back to his parents and to his brothers and sisters. And sooner or later it dawns on the family that the hurt child's siblings are going to make or break the situation. It is their attitudes that provide colour and humour. Family life must become a working situation integrating the need for the stimulation, recognition and safety of the injured member with the more usual demands of children growing up.

Sometimes the baby who comes home will look very normal and begin life by showing a passive sunny disposition; it is more likely, however, that the symptomatic discomforts of having an injured brain will make the infant vociferous in complaint. If one's digestion is poor and one cannot suck well although hungry, or if one is eternally fighting for breath (without anyone being very conscious of one's trouble), then being a baby is not very congenial. Besides, this brain injury usually messes up the immune system which means a constant flow of coughs, colds, and respiratory infection.

The parents and the baby have, of course, just been sent home to get on with things as best they may. There is no counselling or co-counselling with other parents beforehand, no homemaker arriving every morning to help them settle in. Even a social worker is provided at the discretion of the consultant involved. One mother I interviewed had a baby with an ectopic bladder (which in a lay woman's terms meant that the baby's abdomen was split from the genitals to the navel). She was sent home and told to manage as best she could. Her son cried day and night because it is not pleasant to have a split belly. When she took him to the doctor and explained that she was afraid to bathe him, the GP said, 'Gosh, I've never met this before, you'll just have to cope.'

Shattered or depressed as the parents possibly are, solutions appear only as tranquillizers for the mother and phenobarbitone for the baby. (The father's work, if he has any, is usually regarded as sufficient therapeutic diversion from the tragedy.)

Some parents hesitate in explaining their baby's probable disability to their other children. This is reasonable if there are no immediate problems, but if the new baby cries all night, has fits or necessitates the mother's constant departure to hospital, the other children are going to suspect things are not all as they should be and ask questions. Also, since the parents have been through a series of traumatic experiences, their attitude to the baby or to his siblings is not going to be quite normal.

Often the parents have so little idea of what is actually wrong with the baby they can't explain much, even to older siblings. These children are going to react differently depending upon a number of factors, not least their own character and how they have been affected by the priorities and expectations of their parents. If parents have placed a lot of emphasis on material things and have tended to judge by appearances, then the chances are that so will their children. Imagine a professional family used to elegant clothes and intellectual conversation. They plan a family of two bright children who will reflect their own success and be loved and admired by everyone. The first baby is all that can be expected and simply gorgeous, and after two years here comes his prospective playfellow. He too is beaming and bonny – and Down's Syndrome. Well, at least they know where they are, or do they? The capacities of a child injured in this way are variable and depend not only on the degree of injury but the degree of respect and stimulation he gets. And who is going to give that stimulation? Why, the parents and, of course, the other child or children. Whatever happens, life will not be quite the same again. For better or for worse, this fact has to be acknowledged. Degrees of altruism depend on circumstances and what the family has to lose.

I wanted to talk both to sibs who had grown up and to those who were still young. Every age was clearly important. I contacted all the friends I had made who had handicapped children with sibs and those who worked in charities supporting handicapped children. I sent letters to newspapers and magazines advertising my intentions. As the news spread, people wrote or called me up offering to discuss their experiences or to organize small meetings of parents and children. Sometimes I chatted to children at play centres or informally at their homes, often in the midst of animals and toys. The friendliness and courage of everyone I spoke to impressed me greatly.

I was also fortunate to be put in touch with two notable researchers into sibs' lives, Duncan Guthrie and Pauline Fairbrother. I include quotations from their sources which, because they were often anonymous, add an edge to some of the more complex problems sibs have to face. After careful reflection I have decided to do the conventional thing and change people's names.

One eighteen-year-old sibling from an upper-class family evidently dug her heels in early when asked if she would look after her brother in later life. She said, 'I maintain now what I said when I was five. I will look after his stocks and shares but not him.'

People choose different life styles. Few survive without regrets. Siblings are caught because the responsibility is theirs whether they will or no. There is no sharing the problem with the neighbourhood, the school or the church. Either you do what is needed willingly or you do it resentfully, or you don't do it and feel guilty. And perhaps you feel guilty anyway – after all, you are fit. You can find no real satisfaction in apportioning blame because it's nobody's fault.

Now, it is interesting here to compare some statistics on siblings from different income brackets which were collected by Duncan Guthrie. When asked whether their relationship with their hurt member could be described as very caring, 4.5 per cent of upper-class siblings and 4.7 per cent of clerical-class siblings agreed that it was. This compares with the considerably higher 30 per cent of working-class siblings who acknowledged their relationship to be very caring.

I can put forward one more set of statistics from the same source. When asked if the siblings felt that they had become nicer or nastier as a result of living with an individual with a handicap, 59.7 per cent of the upper-class kids and 51.9 per cent of the clerical class said they were nicer. Only 20 per cent of the working class agreed to improvement. And while 2.2 per cent of the upper-class kids and 2.8 per cent of the clerical said it had made them nastier, none of the working-class sibs felt they were less pleasant. The majority of working-class respondents to the questionnaire, 80 per cent, estimated they had stayed the same.

Apparently, a handicapped child has a kind of professional vocation to uplift the lives of those who might otherwise have succumbed to materialism. But why are the working-class sibs better able to make it with their problematic brother or sister?

143

If you've been coping with dirt and noise and the constant crises that come with not enough incomings and too many outgoings, if you've been used to watching your mum struggle and used to pulling your weight because you had to, a handicapped baby is not going to make that much difference. The sense of family is still high among the working class and caring for family is more enduring than money. The furniture is already a bit kicked about and the wheelchair doesn't look that offensive as it squashes into the living-room. If your kid brother gets violent and breaks a few plates, they were Woolworth's not bone china. And as for your own expectations, well, the other two who have left school are only on the dole . . . At least having the kid in the wheelchair to look after is some sort of career. And anyway there's something about him, he's clever despite the way he looks when he's dribbling.

The working-class parents are realistically not full of high academic expectation for their children. This doesn't mean they don't encourage potential when they see it. Gary might have Down's and look a bit odd but he is a loving son and a brother you can rely on.

It would seem that in sibs' ability to cope, the upper class has the hardest time of it. With the middle class the outcome depended upon the parents' character while the working class managed best because traditionally they always had to.

All three groups obviously want help. The upper class have to recognize the truth of the old saying 'Money doesn't buy happiness'. The working or unemployed class who have no lack of the stuff that can't be bought, nevertheless need help with other basic matters such as food, clothing and heating. The middle class long to feel less isolated by the conventions that do not admit handicap. All three groups desperately need more information. If they got together they'd make the kind of team that produces change . . .

But we were just getting the handicapped baby home. One factor must be remembered: however much the infant's consultant has likened him to a cabbage, there is no actual correspondence. He is a person and he is firstly and foremost a person to his siblings. This doesn't mean he will be altogether welcome as a consumer of parental time and energy. Nevertheless, it is vital that he is validated as a person if he is going to recognize himself as one.

If the parents need comfort, the siblings will often try to provide it. Children do have remarkable reserves of energy and understanding but they have to be allowed to be involved if this is going to mature.

Marie's brother Tom came home from hospital in an atmosphere of love and normality. His injury was Down's but his sister Marie thought him very beautiful. Her parents were anxious that both children should feel special. She can remember no jealousy. She simply adored having someone else to love.

Girls can identify with their mother, which provides them with the role of carer and comforter. Christine was eleven when her three-month-old brother John was damaged by the whooping cough vaccination. From that time she saw herself as a young mother. The worst times she can remember were at 2 a.m. when she was woken by her mother. 'Quick, we're off to hospital – John's had one of his turns.' Christine's school work went downhill until John was provided with an oxygen cylinder at home.

Cathy was at the hospital when her baby sister was born. She writes: 'I walked in and the doctor told me that my sister was a Down's Syndrome baby. At first I didn't know what that was and then the doctor told me. I just sat down and looked at my mum. Ten minutes later the doctor came back and he said to my mum and dad, "Do you want to keep her?" My mum said, "Yes, I love her." When my sister came home I kept crying. It took me six weeks to get over it. I kept thinking it was all God's fault. It took me about two weeks to tell my friends.'

What the doctor told Cathy does not appear to have had an ideal effect. And any doctor who can ask 'Do you want to keep her?' in the middle of an obviously intimate family situation will not get high marks for tact.

Sixteen-year-old Agnes remembered the bleak contrast between the eagerly anticipated news of her new baby sister and her parents' explanation of the handicap. 'I felt shattered, depressed and worried. I just couldn't believe it. I felt frustrated that I couldn't cuddle her or treat her like a normal baby. But I also felt more for her. My love grew intensely.'

The five-year-old daughter of a teacher said, 'I was very sorry when they told me, he's my best friend.'

'The young,' said Oscar Wilde, 'know everything.' It is true that while they are young, before their values have had a chance to become rigid, they have an intuitive grasp on a world which defeats adult comprehension. And because they intuit more they are less afraid.

I was once given a book of illustrations and poems by children under thirteen.

'Read them,' my friend said, 'and when I tell you where they were written you'll cry.'

I obeyed. 'They're impressive,' I said. 'Full of insights, optimistic and funny but also very wise. I imagine every one went on to be a poet?'

'They were written by Jewish children in Auschwitz concentration camp. They all went to the gas chambers.'

I closed my eyes, tears ran down my cheeks. I felt a mixture of anger and grief but also a kind of awe. These were ordinary children in an extreme situation. They were like your kids. We try and hide our fears about the mysteries of birth and death from children, forgetting that while they are young they understand them better than we do.

An older sibling can cultivate as fine a sense of the absurd as a three-year-old. Humour of course is best when it is insight shared, and since the siblings are going to live with and shoulder the extra responsibility of caring, they should be allowed the privilege of belly laughter and a little healthy conceit in their abilities.

Parents make a vital difference here, as do support groups. There's nothing like knowing someone else with direct experience. Jill emphasizes this point: 'I was lucky my family belonged to Kith and Kids. My mother once heard me at the age of ten boasting to the other kids that my sister was more handicapped than theirs. Another sibling countered it by claiming that his brother could spit further than anyone else, to be answered by another sister that her brother could be sick more often than anyone else. Where else could we boast about such things? Only with people who shared the same experiences.'

Mary, a South London girl, wrote: 'Strangely, I distinctly remember feelings of pride that my little brother was different from everyone else's. I remember saying "retarded" rather than "handicapped" because it sounded posher.'

Here the injured party conferred distinction rather than disgrace. The writer didn't feel that her nose was pushed out of joint. She had a superior variety of brother.

Another sibling overheard the adults talking about Bill's problems from which he deduced that Bill was 'red handicapped'. He boasted knowledgeably to his friends, 'Bill is special because he's got a Red Handicap.'

Without the pride and the humour the early responsibility can be very wearing. 'In addition to protecting Annie I had to do all I could to act grown up. Being grown up meant not crying, taking care of myself and most important of all being very patient with Annie.'

One mother quoted her small son: 'They are amazed at how grown up I can be and start expecting too much of me – after all, I'm only six. I can't be sensible all the time.'

Another boy remembers his role as 'Someone who was always around to help care for Roger. My father called me his "good night arm". Roger himself called me "Daddy" ... I never felt I dressed like a child, I never felt I knew how to act as a boy. I was a little man.'

Sometimes, but as we have seen not always, the boys were more likely to be left out of things. Girls cast themselves easily as carers and could share. Their brothers saw the hurt child as an even greater rival for their mother's love and escaped as much involvement as possible, locking their feelings away. This could happen if there were an elder boy and girl sibling in the same family. The girl would accept the role as second mother as an extension of her own imaginary games. The boy cut himself off, paying for his detachment in later years. However, if the only help around was a son, whether older or younger, he invariably shouldered all responsibilities as ably as a sister.

Within the family there is slow and steady learning. Whatever postulate they may have made as they embraced their angel with the broken wing, a desire to mend the wing still nags. And it is impossible to keep the doctor's advice to treat each day as it comes with no thought to the future. The task has been set. We are back in the fairytale. Princes and princesses must roll up their sleeves and get into the kitchen.

When six-year-old Toby's brother was born he hoped for a companion a little different from his handicapped elder sister. Jake spent a lot of time in hospital.

There was fear and trembling in Toby's face. 'Is the baby going to die?'

'No, Toby,' reassured his mother.

'Is it drett down (meaning broken)?'

He was told gently that this was so.

'What made it drett down, Mummy? Why are Miriam and Jake drett down?'

Carole explained the difference between Miriam's forceps injury and the mystery which still surrounds Jake's.

The doctor had talked in Toby's presence, apparently above his head. Now the boy wanted to know all the doctor's terms.

The doctor predicted death but his mother said Jake would be all right. Whom should he trust? When he wants to be sure of something he asks her, 'Mummy, will you *promise* it will be like that.'

Siblings are ordinary children working in extraordinary circumstances. When we had child labour the factory owners raked in the profit.

These children take the roles of nurse, teacher, playleader, therapist, counsellor, child minder whether they will or no. Whether the experience enhances or embitters them, it is inescapable.

CHAPTER 9

The Way Sibs Cope

Let us take a closer look at the way sibs cope. Their response will be affected first by their parents and then by their school and friends and beyond. Young children are not too bound by conventions, they will be more open to differences between people and easily appreciative of the individual beneath the handicap. As they grow older the situation becomes more complicated. They cannot avoid the contrast between the values that made up their formative years and those of the society around them.

We all tend to presume we have much the same picture of the world. If we gave one another a little extra time we would discover that we had rather more and rather less in common than we'd thought. From their early days sibs have given their hurt brothers and sisters plenty of time. They are their best motivators. They understand the experience of what it's like to be handicapped more closely than anybody.

It will be helpful to us to try to get under the skin of a brain-injured child. When toddlers are pulling the place apart they're going about the very serious business of learning. Children don't grow up simply from the inside. If you haven't put your infant on a horse every day of his early life, he won't be riding cross-country when he's six. If you are crazy enough to put a perfectly healthy baby into a darkened room and merely feed it, its nervous system will be severely retarded. The recipe for healthy brain development is good interaction with the environment. This is extremely difficult if you happen to be stuck in a wheelchair. Moreover, you have very little hope of knowing what vision of the world to agree upon if your senses continually play you false. Relating to your well brother or sister is your main chance. If you are blind, you must listen. If you are deaf, you must watch. If you are both blind and deaf, you must touch. If you are paralysed, you must do your best with your other senses. There again, perhaps you have any one of a number of visual, auditory or tactile problems no one has seriously identified – sounds echo, you have double vision and your fingers feel as if they are permanently inside thick gloves. You need to use all your intelligence to make as much as you can of this abounding input of chaos. Supposing your problems are largely those of comprehension. The situation is not necessarily that the data isn't being dealt with, it's that so little meaningful stuff is getting through. If you do badly in IQ tests designed for evaluating very different perceptual faculties, it's hardly surprising. Put the psychologist in the same situation and let her try to assess herself. Your attempts to make this known, together with all other serious essays in communication, end with socially undesirable grunts and dribbles. As your acquaintance backs off, you wonder whether these results are worth the original effort.

Apart from wrestling with any number of diverse symptoms, your health is never that good. You have continuous chest infections and colds. Your twisted or paralysed limbs get sore, your digestion is generally lousy and you feel frequent nausea. You hate the mentally cloying effects of the drugs you are given. Although you can observe the differences between yourself and your sibs, you can't actually grasp what it feels like to be healthy or mobile or quick to get your word in.

When you wake up in the morning after having fits and fighting for breath all night, your thoughts turn to your sib. Children like things 'larger than life'. A child whose senses are deprived in any way is desperate for live entertainment. Whatever his sib does, it will be much jollier to witness than anything his parents could do.

In return, the sib, more than anyone else in the world, is going to come to the commendable conclusion that however weak and helpless her handicapped kin is, he's actually tough. The next step is to conclude that he could do more for himself if he was given a bit more of a chance. (Despite the effort and discomfort, the more you do for yourself the better your prospects.)

A baby, sustained by its intuition, investigates unknown terrains with remarkable confidence. The toddler perceives people as individuals. Unaware of convention she is without prejudice. She simply wants to learn more about everything. You need information before you can start making comparisons. Once you have enough, evaluation is unavoidable. This is how Jack put it:

'I think I first noticed the difference between us when I was about five. I knew we would both be starting school that year. (Steven was nearly eight and autistic.) I had the realization that there was something wrong about Steven but I didn't know what it was. The neighbours' children would ask me, "What class is your brother in?" This made me feel uncomfortable. But I knew that Steven had this problem and there was nothing I could do about it.'

Another sibling talked less comfortably about her Down's Syndrome brother.

'David is the eldest in our family. I am three years younger than him. But he hasn't felt like an elder brother since I was three and he came to collect me from school on his trike.'

Questions bubble up.

'When *is* Mary going to feed herself, Mummy?'

'Why can't Phillip play football?'

If your expectations have been undermined, there are sometimes surprises, as Cathy discovered.

'I thought my sister would not be able to talk because she was Down's but she can say "mum", "dad", "ball" and "no". When I go home from school I sometimes take her up to my room – she means a lot to me and my mum.'

Fortunately, whatever the consultant may have predicted, most sibs will go on trying to stimulate their brothers and sisters unless they are forcibly prevented from doing so. They do, after all, want to have fun with this kid. He's their kid. And he will prefer being dragged across the floor bump, bump, bump than being tidily fastened into a corner seat. This is a scenario better imaginable in a working-class kitchen than an upper-class drawing room where the furniture acquired to restrain poor Jim is often considered more aesthetic than Jim unbound.

I remember Doran's total delight in being 'rough-housed' by Lili's friends. Sibs do their best to bring hope and humanity into operation. They hate deathliness and morbidity. They know that you can never go back. You have to push on.

The parents' road is not the siblings'. An agonized mother suffers for both her children:

'Tilly was six when Lynne, then two, started having fits. We were gradually realizing that Lynne was very slow and backward and not doing the normal things her sister had done. Then the fits became more frequent and violent. Frightening enough for a parent to see, let alone a young girl. I can hear Tilly's voice ringing in my ears – "Mummy, please don't cry – I can't help it." '

Tilly is almost certain to be far less afraid of Lynne's seizures than her mother. She will have gathered that if Lynne is having all these fits and surviving, it is because she is tough. Behaviour that remains outrageous to an adult can be taken philosophically by a child.

Graham is also six. Both his brother and sister have serious neurological problems, one symptom of which is seizures. 'I know when Paul's fitting,' he says. 'I call Mum. I saved Hazel when she was fitting in the bath. I like to check up on them both all the time.'

Parents carry regret for the child that might have been. For the other children their brother or sister is the person they know and that's it.

Our addiction to what is 'normal' means that most parents of handicapped children feel isolated. If this eats into them they run the risk of becoming bitter and then the mutual respect between the members of the family breaks down. Siblings well or hurt cease to be heeded. Mandy says: 'Just as soon as I was big enough to take care of Sheila, that's what I had to do; the minute I got home from school, all free time, all holidays. If I went to play with anyone I had to take her along. I was so heartily sick of Sheila. I hated her.'

Presumably Mandy's parents didn't listen to her protests because they felt betrayed by God and Man. Sheila had cut them off from life and her sister was paying for it.

People who are alone are bereft of a yardstick. Mothers can easily become obsessed with the triumphs of the hurt child. A small boy remembered: 'The first time I got all 'A's' on my report card I came running through the front door and Mum was excited so I thought that she already knew. I said, "Mum, I got all 'A's'." And she said, "Oh, that's nice. Guess what? Your brother said his first word today!"'

This was not a happy coincidence. The son is deeply hurt although he doesn't complain. His mother has been at home all day. She is seeking validation. No one else will tell her her work is paying off.

Time and again the sibling will parent his parents. A ten-year-old girl I interviewed said, 'I'd like more time with my mother. I have to look after her when she's tired. My wish for my mummy is I'd just like to make her happy.'

While the children are eager to do something, to get some result, the father can founder on his new responsibility. He is not always emotionally prepared to watch his wife feed the kid in the wheelchair before she feeds him. He cannot always unbend enough to share the nappy changing and lifting and carrying and all the extra attendant domesticity that takes its unvarying course year in, year out.

There is no special counselling for him. Indeed, he might initially resist it, seeing it as a reflection of his own inadequacy. Fathers who take this problem in their stride or who struggle to give what is needed with their love increase the family's interior and exterior strength. You admire these men because they have dug deeply into themselves. They have a lightness as well as a determination about them.

The child who has decided not to cry or demand but to care and take pride in the status of carer is aware when father does not come up to scratch.

'My dad always loses his temper.'

'My father reacted very badly, resulting in alcoholism and the family splitting up.'

'My father couldn't accept Jack's disability and left my mother but after he'd gone life was normal.'

'My sister has Down's and it has been difficult concerning my father and us over the years due to lack of acceptance on his part.'

The result of this is the emergence of a relatively high proportion of single-parent families in which the responsibilities of the father are divided between mother and siblings.

The government is not God and is under no obligation to honour good works. Siblings don't get high marks in school for their social service. The chances are that they fall behind. Our society retains certain priorities; spending money, not giving time, is what helps the economy go round. For many of these sibs the personal has already become the political. Their experience makes them think about and contrast values.

Whether the injured child is mobile or in a wheelchair, the aesthetics of the house are bound to have altered. Degrees of poverty will make their contribution; so will a child who is always clumsy or who has violent 'temper tantrums'. A wheelchair has to be dragged over carpets. It thumps into doors and skirting boards and people's ankles . . .

Sibs' attitudes to this state of affairs may vary with their age and sex. Here is a sib's forthright description of lunch with her handicapped brother: 'He eats bits and pieces of this and that and chucks the rest. He licks the tomato sauce off the sandwich and chucks the sandwich. My mother's floor was always a mess.'

We could conclude that her brother's digestion must be terrible and his palate blurred by drugs and nausea. He probably doesn't chew very well. Getting him to eat anything at all seems like a victory.

A girl whose brother regularly breaks things up despaired: 'I'm ashamed of the plastic cups and shabby furniture at home.'

Often sibs are reluctant to bring their friends back once they've become aware of the state of the house. The downstairs rooms may not be quite perfect, but what of the bedrooms? A child who numbers incontinence among his disabilities is haunted by a faint odour of urine and sour breath even in open spaces. The little bunk bedroom he shares with his brother or sister does not retain its charm long. One sib who had to share a bedroom with her brother Andrew told me:

'He used to scream all night. I could sleep through it a lot. But . . . I do like pretty things. I'd have a soap collection and he'd throw it about the room. I used to cry but you couldn't blame him.' Soap wasn't all. Andrew was doubly incontinent. 'He'd begin chucking smelly things even in my hair.' She said this with remarkable cheerfulness as she sat in her new house with the pretty things at last all around. 'I'm very house proud now. When I was at home it was no use worrying about it so you didn't notice.'

Excrement in the hair can be a way of life. Humour occurs because in extreme circumstances the things you thought mattered suddenly become ridiculous. If your child was drowning in muddy water, would you bother about your smart clothes when you were pulling her out? And when you hugged her safe in your arms and someone said, 'But look at your hair, it's positively squalid', what would you do? Well, no one would mind if you laughed. The circumstances of a chronically hurt child are like this all the time. Sibs accommodate it to an incredible degree. They perform the life-saving act routinely. The sibs I spoke to were not denigrating their nearest and dearest when they told me:

'My favourite toy is Lego but Carl eats it. He'll just champ his way through anything.'

'He likes to chew something – even the table.'

'You can't take him anywhere where he might damage something.'

This may not necessarily be mindless behaviour. It could be a sensually deprived kid trying to collect vital information.

'Why do you think he bites things?'

'Because he just has to get his teeth into something.'

'He enjoys it.'

'I think it's because he feels frustrated.'

'Does it embarrass you?'

'No, but it might when I'm older.'

'There's nothing wrong with Carl. He's just different. There's nothing wrong with being different.'

This is true in theory; it has its drawbacks in practice. Holidays were a thorny problem. Sometimes it was hard to admit you never really had one.

'Not this year.'

'Last year?'

'No, my mum wasn't well enough.'

The business of taking the whole roadshow away somewhere else is about as wild as can be imagined. Sue's family took one holiday in Devon when she was six. After this her mother's fears for Andrew's safety meant that although they talked about holidays, they never actually took any.

'On two occasions we were all at the door ready to leave when Mum broke down and said she had a migraine and couldn't go through with it. We kids started crying. We didn't blame Andrew, we blamed Mum for starting the migraine.'

A loving father will tramp miles with a small injured child on his back so that everyone gets across the headland and down to the sea. Siblings put the responsibility for a good holiday squarely on their parents. Holidays are magical events. Children talk about them for months before and months afterwards. They confer status. If you have not been anywhere or done anything when you come back after the summer break you are automatically demoted. You listen to the spectacular tales of your peers and endeavour to keep your pride and dignity with a plausible excuse or an outright lie. If your parents do risk the adventure, few would embrace the social contract of an hotel. Usually it's self-catering flats. A change is as good as a rest they say, and a mother has to believe it to survive.

As everyone grows older there is a curiosity about the normal household. Anything that escapes reference to a handicapped child has the label 'normal'. A salient factor of normal life is time to do what you want to do without the least little bit of guilt. But perhaps what is normal ceases to be so wonderful when you find that the kids from the normal household along the street are somewhat less than magnanimous in their kindness and understanding.

Sue found that as Andrew grew up and his problems were clearer, the teasing began in earnest.

'Your brother's a div, yah!'

When Marie was twelve she began taking Tom to play in the park.

'As we went down a street in what you'd call a nice middle-class area, the children playing there began to mimic his walk and started shouting. Tom didn't pick it up. When we'd passed I remember crying out of grief for him.'

'I got angry when people stared at Frances. I felt there was a stigma attached to me as well.'

Siblings realize that children from families whose every member possesses a mind and body of harmonious clock-work demonstrate no humility in respect of this great advantage. It is our nature to take things for granted. Having handicapped kinsfolk won't win you sympathy, admiration or status. You quickly realize that jeers rather than cheers will meet your stories of domestic heroism. Indifference runs a close second and you begin to appreciate it. A boy whose sister has spina bifida quickly clammed up on the subject because 'the vast majority of my friends would find it extremely humorous'.

Most of us can remember the pattern. Children who laugh at other kids' disadvantages are not irredeemably callous. It is fear that causes them to throw open their mouths and pump their lungs, while the child who is different buries his face. We are all afraid of the unknown. If you drive round the corner and find a gruesome car accident, whatever you do, unless you are well informed about first aid, your instinct is to run away. This is not callous. Unlike babies, we have learned to fear new events rather than to trust ourselves to enquire into them. We need to be better informed. Given a good balance of information and intuition we can usually come up with something. Until then we like to keep ourselves and our children away from exposure to disagreeable subjects. The law assists this in the case of criminals and the mentally ill: they lock them up. The symptoms of brain injury, diverse and misunderstood as they frequently are, have begun to appear increasingly in the community. Hurt babies grow up and the bigger they get, the more frightening they become.

Graham was delighted when two little boys from his prep school finally expressed a wish to come home for tea. The boys were weekly boarders and asked permission of their house teachers. Their house teachers refused. They could not be held responsible for the shocking effect a close encounter with two diagnosed cabbages might have on schoolboy minds. Once Graham's fellow pupils lost this chance of enlightenment they retreated into the safe heights of their superior 'normality' to pelt him with commonplace abuse. It is not easy to attempt the conversion of one's mates under such conditions. However, observation of apparently normal families can be surprising.

A twelve-year-old girl remarked: 'When Joanne was born I felt sad and rather sorry that I should have a handicapped sister and everyone else had a normal brother or sister, but they seem to hate their brothers and sisters whereas I do not.'

More insight comes from Clare: 'I used to think how nice it would be if I had a normal brother and our family was normal like all my friends' families. But after a while I realized that everyone thought that their families were weird.'

We conspire to pretend to be the same in order to hide our differences. We are all much more interesting than we let on, as any journalist for a Sunday tabloid is jubilantly aware. Laugh at yourself with indecent frequency and you will develop the knack of digesting the variegated colours of this world rather than choking on them.

Kids laugh at themselves, adults create embarrassment and stop them, thus they laugh at other people instead. Gentler siblings become isolated or bullied at school. Toughies may manage to stand up for themselves and their kin but the threat of ridicule remains.

Jake, an adolescent trying to cope with a home severely disrupted by the bizarre behaviour of his non-communicating brother, continually gets it in the neck from his class-mates. 'You're as bad as your barmy kid.'

School drops one in at the deep end: 'It never really occurred to me that there was anything unusual about my sister until I started school and heard the jokes.'

'Man cannot bear too much reality!' Most of us are cultivated sleepwalkers who should be woken up sympathetically by degrees. Sibs get a boost up the ladder towards higher consciousness and it hurts. Some do find that the constant obligations of the sib are less of a bond and more of a bind. These avoid their classmates' ridicule by pre-empting it.

'I tell my friends how she annoys me and makes me feel rotten.'

'I tell them how terrible she is.'

In the right context, letting off steam is a healthy way to get rid of suppressed emotion. Human beings are, however, contradictory and those classmates who might otherwise have teased you about your 'divi' brother can suddenly begin to take his side and start exhorting you to be more loving. You can push guilt out of your day-to-day thoughts but it remains below the surface niggling away, taking the edge off pleasure. You need time with your parents to sort matters out, and somehow it is rarely possible.

Small incidents swell out of all proportion. Children remember them later and are still unsure of their interpretation.

'Was I cruel?'

'Did I really hurt him?'

'Could I have stopped myself?'

Early adolescence is a critical time. Rebellious youth is confronted with a new and rigorous set of conventions demanded by peers. The assurances of childhood melt under such scrutiny. You know that everywhere you go you will be summed up first by your appearance, then by your style and then by your family.

A fourteen-year-old girl wrote that she could discuss with her parents 'how great it would be if my brother was normal' and with her brothers and sisters 'how normal it would be to have a normal younger brother'. Having dealt with the negative side she could then go out cheerfully to chat to her friends about all the things he did 'that made him good fun to play with'.

How do kids judge how much internal strife is part of normal family life and how much is the direct result of their brother or sister being to a greater or lesser degree unusual?

Sibling rivalry is normal – so are the swings of loving and hating.

Children's lives abound in extremes and adults must be careful not to judge them by adult standards. When a grown-up says 'I don't like him', it implies a complete and final evaluation. When a child says 'I don't like you' she means at *this* precise minute. A child is used to growing and changing so fast he's hardly the same person ten minutes hence. One should treat a child as an equal but not as an adult. The family that condemns or deters the sib from telling her hurt brother that she doesn't like him could change a transient response into a guilty secret which is a pretty unbearable thing to have to drag around.

A family with a hurt child cannot blithely imagine 'it won't happen to us' because it already has. The illusion of the good life is swept away for ever. However far siblings try to run from the fact of their position, it will pursue them.

'The worst act of disowning I did was not to invite him to my wedding. I still haven't forgiven myself.'

What you fear is not your brother or sister's demanding unorthodox behaviour but the breakdown of your own self-image. Turn and face this imagined enemy, make it your friend, and salvation is yours. This seems hard to achieve alone (although some children effortlessly manage it). Siblings have their wits about them and they work exceptionally hard. Their observations have been kept bottled up, so have their emotions; they long for a hearing. We can learn from what they have to say.

CHAPTER 10

——◆——

You Are Your Brother's Teacher

At this stage I want to focus in more detail on the contribution of a group of sibs. Some are older and can view their situation with hindsight. Others are still very much in the middle of things. All of them made it clear that growing up with a hurt brother or sister had given them different priorities from their peers. Family life may aspire to be the same as the neighbours' but that very aspiration draws attention towards another kind of consciousness. They know that their hurt kin affects every decision that is made in the household and will continue doing so for the rest of their lives.

The degree to which many siblings develop their roles as carers made me feel I had come across a stratum of hidden genius. After all, the goodness in the world is founded upon the qualities of our domestic relationships and our private acts. Governments make news but human kindness is what makes life worth living.

Yet whoever heard of a sib boasting to his mates about his genius for homemaking? Kids learn to esteem the things that other people value. The boy-hero is found on the interplanetary battlefield – not struggling to feed his handicapped sister on the kitchen floor.

In my research for this book I met children whose view of life was constantly dominated by living intimately with brothers and sisters in need of help. But outside of their particular families, appreciation of the job they did or why they were doing it remained negligible.

Kirsteen was eighteen months old when Alistair was born. As a little girl she recognized her young brother was slow and appointed herself his teacher, protector and translator.

'I always knew what he wanted. Alistair'd do anything for me and almost nothing for anyone else. With just Mum he'd refuse to go out and sit and watch TV all day.'

Kirsteen would rush home from school to grab her adoring pupil. If he was cross and exasperated she could empathize and calm him down.

The art of restoring an individual's good nature is not to criticize him because he *is* a problem but to let him see that you are aware that he genuinely *has* one. Being angry because you can't do what you want to is quite normal and certainly not unintelligent. It could well be an incentive to achieve. To be told that your justifiable rage is merely an irrational temper tantrum does not help. Brothers and sisters are perfectly well aware of what it feels like when the adult world refuses to take you seriously. In one sense the hurt kid acts out the less obvious frustrations of his well sib, who may try to explain.

'Mummy, he's just angry. You have to understand I could kick and scream when I can't get my drawing right but I don't. I *tell* you about it.'

Kirsteen didn't pity Alistair.

'When he was eight he chewed up half my stamp collection. I think it was the bright colours. He threw the other half out of the window because he heard us coming and panicked – he knew I'd be furious.'

This child teacher wasn't perfect although she was tenacious: 'Two years later I was fooling about on his trike and I broke it. I forgot that no one expected him to ride a bike. I felt so bad I told him he could share my two wheeler and I'd teach him to ride it. There was no alternative then – he had to learn.'

Before dark, a bruised but triumphant Alistair was an independent cyclist.

Kirsteen became a teacher of handicapped children. 'If your experience is seen by others as positive,' she says, 'then you will treat it as such. I became deeper and more self-aware because of Alistair.'

Marie has a brother Tom who is about three years younger than she is. He has Down's Syndrome. When the baby came home she says, 'I thought, gosh, this is my new companion. How beautiful he is!' Marie was not a born teacher. She was a highly sensitive little girl very eager to love.

Perhaps without Tom as he was, life would have been harder for Marie. If your nature is an unusually giving one, the rest of the world is more likely to take you for an idiot than a saint. But Marie could pour her love into Tom, knowing it was well received. Her parents separated and her mother became the music teacher at her primary school. Being teacher's daughter only increased the bullying she got from the other kids because she wasn't a toughie. She cried easily and couldn't retaliate either by actions or words. Relief came when Tom's school holidays clashed with the term and he arrived bonny and snug in his buggy.

'I was very proud and explained everything to the others. They all flocked round. They said, "Ooh, isn't he lovely", because he looked so small and cuddly. I wished he would come every day because he made me important – I could say "This is my brother" like everyone else in class who had brothers and sisters. I did wish Tom was at the same school as me.'

Thus without undue effort Tom became a popular hero. The intuitive rapport between the pair remained strong even during his periods of frustration. Learning to bear even minor limitations you don't understand isn't easy. By seven, Tom was throwing food everywhere and refusing all meals except toast and Marmite with yogurt for his pudding. When he was taken out by bus, which he could safely anticipate he would be every day, he relieved his feelings by pulling the hair of the passengers seated in front of him.

As sibs grow up, their responsibilities increase. In the case of Marie and Tom it can begin as desirable adventure.

'I felt confident,' she said. 'People were always so under-standing when my mother was with us. But it was very different the first time I was alone on the bus in charge of Tom.' The fat bald-headed chap who had just had the last vestiges of his precious hair pulled didn't pause for explanations. The full force of his fury descended upon Marie. 'I apologized over and over again but the man stormed off the bus. I felt sick all the way home because I was afraid it would always be like this when Tom and I were out by ourselves.'

In fact Tom's next attempt to grab at a head of hair in the seat in front of him was his last.

Marie explained: 'He was dangling a gorgeous blonde wig. The lady tried to snatch it off him but Tom wanted to put it back fast. You could see from the astonishment and horror on his face he was determined to pretend the whole thing hadn't happened. The bus driver who'd watched the struggle in his driving mirror pulled over to the side of the road. We wondered what for. He had to laugh. He couldn't hold it in. Soon all the passengers started laughing, even the woman, and I realized it was going to be all right.'

There are organizations like Contact a Family which promote play schemes for a mixture of handicapped children and sibs. Sibs can find each other or, like Marie, they begin to realize their potential for relationships in other ways.

'I found it easier to mix there,' she said. 'I'd enjoyed school work but not the loneliness. Although the other sibs were fun, I played more and more with the handicapped children and as time went by I sensed they were growing to love me too. I began to realize I could be good at communication.'

Because Marie can look through to Tom's essential nature, which overrides the difficulties posed by his injury, their support can be mutual. 'I find it comforting to put my arms round his neck, he gives me strength. I admire him terribly. He's very patient now, it was an effort for him. I couldn't be so patient.

'People say he's abnormal and imperfect but to me he is perfect in so many ways. When I feel sad what I need most is love and that's what Tom gives me.'

The siblings I talked to were very different in character. Kirsteen was warm and brisk, Marie gentle and intuitive. Christine was firm and down-to-earth in her affections. Her eldest brother was killed when he was four. A third child was stillborn. John arrived amid great rejoicing. Despite his severe brain injury after a routine whooping cough vaccination, she says:

'I remember thinking he was a bright child and a trier. At home he was a whirlwind at jigsaws. Then from the first day at school they did nothing with him and he started going downhill. Mum always disciplined him at home, but they just said, "Oh, he doesn't understand!" So from eleven we had him home.'

Fighting for John meant a constant war with officialdom. There were battles over the large number of drugs John was always prescribed. 'My mum thought they were making him worse and she wouldn't increase the dose. We didn't want a zombie and we weren't having one.' Time and again after winning the fight the mother broke down in her daughter's arms.

'I would get home from school and find her crying. It made me want to run all the way so that she wouldn't be alone.'

Once John left school they planned a diary so that there was always someone to look after him. The unity of this family springs from the relationship between mother and daughter. 'Mum said we shouldn't feel we had to take responsibility,' Christine says. 'We made our choices together. I couldn't see John in a home.' The result is that Christine's husband and children all live together with John and her parents. Her brother continues to be the affectionate Eros round which their world revolves. He cuddles Christine's children like teddy bears. 'There's a lovely way about him,' she says. 'You never feel you're not needed or appreciated.'

John is still deteriorating neurologically. 'Since the encephalogram his walking is worse. He falls over wrinkles in the carpet. His conversation used to be clearer. I remember him telling me when he stole some sausages, now he says "mum mum mum mum" two hundred and fifty times.'

There is no doubt that repeating 'mum mum' over and over is bound to be irritating. Christine passes over this. 'Mind you, we've got to the point where we don't hear "mum mum" any more. We just find out what John means.'

As sibs help their brothers and sisters to grow up, that

early recognition of their resilience seems to fade away. Sooner or later children discover their own vulnerability and the pace of the world which has little time to pay attention to individuals.

Parents too are unusual if they are not over-protective. The more you protect the more poignant becomes the contrast between life inside your home and in the street outside. When classmates sneer and jeer at your kin you retaliate with greater protectiveness. Every sibling I spoke to pointed out the value of having the chance to talk about the situation to their peers. Getting the point over to ordinary children was as important as finding other sibs. The dream is to be totally, absolutely and completely accepted.

Anne was another child who eagerly appropriated her Down's Syndrome brother, Mark.

'He was mine, I loved babies. I would take him out for walks. When he was older we'd play games. I used to pretend to sit on him. I was always proud of my brother except the day when he rolled on the pavement to eat his ice cream.'

In relationships like Anne and Mark's, laughter and tears are always close to the surface. Growing up makes no difference. She knows that Mark is both strong and resilient and extraordinarily vulnerable. As she drives to visit him at a farm school, she sees him in the road. He's evaded his teachers and is heading off home on his own initiative. Weeping, she throws open the door of the car and drags the young man to safety. Mark is bewildered and pleased. Here is the lovely sister he has started off to visit, but why does she cry?

Sue's mother had German measles in the early days of her pregnancy. Her doctor refused to believe that she was carrying a child until it was too late for an abortion. When he was born the nurse told her, 'I'm afraid your son will be blind and deaf and never walk.'

Responsibility for Andrew was assumed by mother and daughter. 'With Andrew,' Sue says, 'you can't help seeing the funny side of things, not always at the time, but we did laugh as well as cry.' She is also very honest. 'Now I've left home I appreciate my mother more. How I wish I hadn't moaned when she asked me to look after him. I never helped her with the washing up. My God, how she coped. Because she came out of it, we all came out of it.'

Sue is two years older than Andrew. Regardless of the initial complaints, once she was out with him nobody put him down unchallenged. 'When I went round with Andrew I'd stick up for him. I've got strong views,' she says, 'and I'm strong-willed.'

Despite the prognosis, Andrew walked at ten and the family felt he could see and hear. Since they had elected to manage him at home they were left to get on with it.

'Andrew's very loving,' Sue said, 'although he often forgets and bites instead of kissing . . . Then I'd be watching telly and he'd creep up and pull my hair. I longed to whack him one – you couldn't really because he wouldn't understand.

'We taught Andrew by pumping things into him. Everything is a routine, the day always ends at 9 p.m. with soup and a bath. He had a great fascination for bricks. I taught him the knack of spinning them. He'd do it with tops too but when they didn't work he'd have the screaming hab dabs. I guessed he always knew more than he'd let on so I got him to do things like his colours. Other people said he couldn't. Mother said, "You've got a gift there . . ."

'In our house you'd never be sure what would happen next. You'd be listening to the radio and then up it would go full blast and the next thing Andrew would be chucking it across the room and the batteries would fly out. I missed out on privacy. My eldest brother had to have a bedroom by himself because of schoolwork so it was me and Andrew. There was a board across our door to stop Andrew from wandering at night. I had to lift it if I wanted to go anywhere. I used to collect little knick-knacks but I was always coming home from school and finding them broken. In the end I just packed in collecting. Mother never let me take anyone up into the room and I'm not surprised because it was so messy.

'Mind you, I felt my parents appreciated me. I aways got what I wanted and I never felt Andrew was the talking point all the time. Mum was very protective. Even when I was twenty-two she wanted me to come into the bedroom and say "I'm home". You could say Andrew helped me find my husband because lots of fellas were easily put off so I began to look for someone deeper. I met Simon organizing a disco party for disabled kids. Do you know, the neighbours actually asked me, "Is your brother going to your wedding?" I said, "He's my brother, isn't he?" I could've said more but they wouldn't have understood.'

Sue reached for her wedding album and there's Andrew in a smart suit standing between his mum and dad endeavouring to keep upright and smile at the same time. 'Every birthday I put myself out for a different toy for him, especially now I've left home. The thing is he breaks stuff so easily. Last birthday I bought him a blow-up bat and ball and I showed him how to hold it and he did it! Whenever I walk in I tend to talk to him a bit silly sometimes, like we used to. I call him Boo and a nice big smile crosses his face and he'll start laughing because I'm there!'

A blow-by-blow account of Sue's early life is pretty strong stuff. But Sue talks with such humour and animation I could see how well she had come out of it.

'I've a lot of patience. It was a toss-up whether I should work with mentally handicapped children or hairdressing. So now I cut the hair of kids who are mentally handicapped because I can move with them. I understand them.

'Andrew,' she says, 'has broadened my mind. I took on a hospital full of incontinent women for hairdressing. It's nothing to me. I was in the middle of washing a lady's hair, we were holding her for the shampoo while her wee dribbled right down my legs.

'When people moan about silly things I say, "Well, if you've got two arms and two legs that's all that matters." It makes me more appreciative. People don't know how lucky they are.'

I discovered that sisters rarely seemed to be able to confide in their brothers. Even exceptionally sensitive brothers more often found it easier to express themselves by actions rather than discuss feelings.

So, when I met a very caring brother I was touched by his willingness to communicate. Tim's elder sister Louise looks so elegant and pretty that it isn't until she begins to speak that you realize the intellectual difficulties she has to contend with. Tim found himself caring more for his sister than going out to play football. Louise herself was no sensitive flower. She was headstrong and self-willed. 'She can scream and shout,' he says, 'and bang the ceiling. When I was about ten and she was twelve, she loved answering the phone. The day I got there first Louise let fly and hit me in the groin. Then while I was lying on the floor moaning, she offered me a chocolate curly whirly.'

Staying in with Louise cannot be described as a soft option. Tim knows he's become over-protective for both of them. 'I wouldn't take her to the pub. It could lead her into bad ways. I do try and avoid trouble. The greatest thing I missed was the acceptance of Louise by other people. Often the young and inexperienced can hurt. I worry about Louise being hurt.'

We all worry about people dear to us, especially family and above all children. If you are close to someone who is vulnerable in so many ways, what can you do? Siblings were full of ideas. At present they are hardly recognized as a group and their individual voices are easily lost.

What they are saying reveals that alongside academic qualifications, the values needed in the classroom (which is where all kids spend a great proportion of their lives) are kindliness towards each other and understanding. If these qualities were given status in all school activities, children would feel less threatened and more open. In consequence they would also become happier because they could use their energies in creating relationships rather than self-defence. Tim repeated the overwhelming view: 'At school only a few close friends knew. If I'd said anything it would have meant nothing to them. I'd like to have discussed Louise with the whole class.'

Fifteen-year-old Helen and nine-year-old Robert have an adopted brother aged six called James. James was two when he arrived with a diagnosis of mental and physical handicap. For reasons that their neighbours on the council estate have not yet fathomed, a perfectly normal healthy happy family went out of its way to saddle itself with the worst misfortune some could envisage. They adopted one of 'those' children. When I met the family they were just in the process of moving house, which upheaval was primarily motivated by James's educational needs. I do not of course know what this household was like before James's arrival but because James was their choice they offered a reaction to his situation in which there was no guilt. James is also the youngest so that neither his brother nor sister could be said to have missed out on their babyhood.

When they first saw James with his foster parents, Helen described him as 'a frightened bird, not as bad as I'd thought'. It took six months for the adoption order to go through. The day I arrived James was at playschool. Robert and Helen were sitting among the packing cases that had gradually swallowed up their possessions. 'We just treat James as normal,' Robert said. 'He doesn't need to talk because he's so good at communicating in other ways.'

Helen said, 'I worked at his school for a year. I prefer doing something for people who really need help.'

Robert handed me a cup of tea. 'James spends hours leaning over the gate but the neighbours ignore him. There's a friend of my mum's who's a nurse who said, "With all my training I wouldn't know how to cope with him." They all think we're a bit daft and we think the same way about them.

'It's hard to sleep with him,' Robert went on blithely. 'He snores but if he's not snoring I rush over and shake him because I think he's stopped breathing. We call him "Chiff Chiff" because his breathing is so bad.

'James gets ill very easily. He used to dehydrate. He's had pneumonia and chicken pox. It's been desperate. He was very ill for a whole week with his temperature in the hundreds. He's a right little fighter.

'You should see the cupboard full of medicine he's got.' Robert pointed to the kitchen. 'He has to take them all twice a day.'

James is due home in half an hour but they get out the photograph album which has been preserved from the tea chests. 'See,' says Helen, 'when we first had him he won a baby competition. We didn't tell them anything about him either.

'Once,' she goes on, 'we tried a holiday without him

but we were constantly wondering where he was. Robert couldn't sleep without him snoring.'

'It's something you get used to,' says Robert. 'And I kept laying his place at meal times and waiting for him to come in.'

The whole family congratulate themselves because James can walk. 'He doesn't like being made to do things,' Helen says, 'but we all know he has to. We've spent four years trying to get him walking and Mum doesn't want him put in the Special Care Unit with the worst handicaps. That's why we're moving.'

Just then James's playgroup van pulls up outside and Robert heads out to meet him.

'We make the neighbours laugh,' says Helen, 'because we always ask James how he is and what he's been doing.'

I don't expect their neighbours would have laughed if they'd heard Robert talking to a dog. Nowadays it's even socially acceptable to talk to plants.

Helen says, 'People always go on about us being brave. I tell them having James doesn't take bravery – he takes a lot of time, a lot of patience and a lot of love.'

Garath is ten and his brother Alex, aged twelve, has Down's Syndrome. They played table tennis at the Saturday club while his mother talked to me.

'Garath has been a great balancer,' she said. 'Everything I did for Alex I did for him because he was handicapped. Then I found I was doing the same things for Garath. He never stops talking. With him it's a normal family. He calls Alex fatty and Alex calls him stinky.'

(Why is it such a relief to hear one's nearest and dearest exchanging these insults?) The pair of them come into the room and start climbing over a stack of huge vinyl blocks. 'I know that Garath is very optimistic about Alex.' She pauses to see if I understand the insecurity of this optimism.

'From the way he talks you can tell that he wants to be sure Alex will have learnt something when he leaves school so that he can go out to work. He feels responsible.'

Garath jumps down and launches into things.

'They don't push Alex hard enough,' he says. 'I think he's often frustrated and alone at times. He needs not to be shoved off when people want a conversation.'

'Do you feel isolated?' I asked.

'I feel different from other boys my own age, sort of strange. It makes me slightly separate from them but I can cope all right, it doesn't get me down.

'Anyway I do things for my mother most children my age don't have the opportunity to do and I like it. For instance, I can get all the shopping out of the way.'

This is an interesting manner of putting it. Are our children wanting extra responsibilities? True responsibility is different from taking orders. It's a chance to be active in decision-making. People want to know your opinion. You can initiate a course of action and get on with it – this is what Garath finds sustaining.

'What about your friends? Do they accept your way of life?' I asked.

'I talked about Alex to friends when I was about eight and some of them made jokes like "He's a bit silly". So I told them the situation and they stopped. Now there's a boy who comes regularly and plays with Alex.'

Garath returns to his game. The vinyl blocks have become a catwalk along which Alex is modelling clothes.

Jane, also ten, has been dressing up her eighteen-year-old sister Sally. Sally looks rather younger than Jane. She flits about with her chin tucked down and her head cocked to one side. She drools almost continuously. You would be forgiven for thinking that she is oblivious of her surroundings but catching sight of her mouth I can see she is smiling.

'I like looking after Sally,' Jane says as she tries her first with a large floppy hat and then a pert flowered one. 'It makes me feel good. She doesn't get me angry – I just have to shout at her when she steals food or dribbles. Sally likes eating most, and I stop her eating the things she shouldn't eat. When we say "Dinner!" she shoots out into the kitchen.'

Jane methodically arranges a chiffon scarf round Sally's shoulders.

'I bought her soap and bubble bath and bubbles on her birthday. I bath with her every Saturday.'

'Do you like that?'

She smiles. 'Yes, we splash each other. Sally can always make me laugh. She can do a head over heels roly-poly on the sofa.'

'What will you do when you grow up?'

'Look after handicapped children so that I'll know what to do with Sally when she's older. My mum worries about Sally's future.'

Martin is nine. Karen thirteen and Neil fifteen. Their seventeen-year-old brother Ian is mentally and physically handicapped. Neil, being closest to him in age, is Ian's main protector. He is a quiet handsome boy who looks several years older than his age.

I realize that to admit concern in the brazen-faced way I'm asking him to is embarrassing in the extreme. Do his friends understand?

'The people who come to the house do. Ian cuddles girls and the girls cuddle him back.'

'No odd reaction?'

'The other day a boy who saw me trying to get Ian up off the floor asked, "What's the matter with your mate?" When I told him Ian was handicapped the boy said, "Why don't you write to that TV programme *Jim'll Fix It*?"'

CHAPTER 11

'I'd Like to Kick Stuart's Head In'

I wonder whether, in describing the lives of these 'other children', I have really communicated the flavour of their extremes of emotion. When sibs say they value their experience, they don't mean they were never irritated or upset. They don't mean they were never angry or frightened. Rather, it is that when they take stock of themselves, there seems to be a lot of good positive substance in their make-up which gives them a strong sense of their own worth.

But there is a dark side. To skip its implications would be foolish, although in the retelling, because life refuses to be quite consistent, you will find comedy mixed with some of the incidents.

When the average parents are asked, 'How are you, and how are the children?' in all probability they answer 'Fine' regardless of how they actually feel.

By contrast, in the world of handicap, where home life is a steady battle against innumerable adversaries, people would actually like to stop and tell you quite a lot about how they were if you had time to listen. An open mind is essential.

If sibs think they're being judged they won't know where to begin because no one part of their story by itself is the truth. The truth is the flavour of the whole and it is being added to each day.

The first big influence on sibs is, very naturally, their parents who have, in their turn, been exposed to society's peculiar incomprehension of the family's needs. Most parents are amazing. Nevertheless, trying to do the right thing can lead to blind desperation.

Twelve-year-old Bernard summed up the despair of his father's and mother's handling of his handicapped elder brother. 'They are always going to extremes, violence met with violence. They never do what I suggest.'

When the failure to communicate has become critical, much depends on whether the necessary emotional, physical or financial help can reach you in time. Anger or tears are only unreasonable if they get out of hand. Most parents manage to keep a balance. Their degree of isolation can be a precipitating factor. Michael and his parents are an example of what can happen when there is nobody to turn to.

'Both my elder brothers were mentally handicapped. Sometimes they'd wander off together into the city without apparent cause or purpose. This drove us to distraction and led to systematic beatings in order to control their behaviour. The memory of violence still brings me out in a sweat ... I have often wondered what sort of person I would have been if I hadn't had two such brothers. I feel that a great store of anger was laid down by the combination of the feeling of the injustice of the double blow: the blind stupidity of a system which appeared unwilling to provide help or to comprehend; the cruelty of strangers and the ignorance of nearly everyone in our environment.'

Michael is writing about his childhood in the forties. It is relevant because although there is more potential help around today, many families still feel similarly neglected.

Besides this, Michael's past experience continues working powerfully in his present.

'Running alongside these memories is a strong emotional tide which I can only indicate by describing a tendency to cry when confronted with images or situations involving children. This brings to the surface an anxiety I have about the normality and vulnerability of my own children.'

Parents struggling to do their best for their children can't always trust their intuition. They have also to base their actions upon the degree of information available at any given time. But what looks best in theory is not always so in fact. Siblings must weather the confusion. One teenage girl explained: 'I can remember endless Sundays in the car going to visit Brian in his residential hospital, Mum and Dad crying all the way home and me still a kid having to comfort them and knowing all the time it was supposed to be for me that they put Brian away in this institution.'

If a sib is asked to sit on his feelings for too long there will be damage in all sorts of ways. David, twelve, has an elder brother Stuart, both physically and intellectually impaired. David hates school. He maintains he's picked on and generally disliked. He gets into fights, his teachers are exasperated with him.

Initially the social worker who chats to David can elicit only glowing reports of his relationship with Stuart. Then suddenly David explodes.

'Actually I'd like to kick Stuart's head in. I'd really like to have a normal brother.' Revelations of injustice flow out. His mother is short-tempered, he is acutely aware that she doesn't want him favoured. He is always told that he should know better than his brother as though not being handicapped should have made him superhuman to make up for Stuart's deficiencies. David always gets it in the neck for doing wrong despite the fact that Stuart is older and ought

The Other Child

(had it not been for his wretched problem) to shoulder the larger portion of blame for their arguments. David's recognition that he should be kind to Stuart wrestles with the nagging fact that his own needs are disregarded. He sees that his parents are reacting superficially towards him. He is liked when he is good and rejected when he isn't. There is never a space in which he can get a hearing. David's feelings towards them fluctuate equally between love when they praise him and hatred when he finds himself unjustly criticized. His parents have imprisoned him within their own guilt. They dare not come out and scream, 'This is Hell.'

It isn't done for ordinary people to 'suffer' publicly. If you have a handicapped child in your family you are expected to pretend it's nothing worse than a head cold. Everything about your life is different from your neighbour's but you are invited to remain respectable by outwardly ignoring it. The absence of an outlet for pain and frustration produces a deep emotional confusion which can lead to guilt. Guilt is the antithesis of personal responsibility. It is an entirely negative emotion which sticks unproductively to its victims, wearing them out by its very uselessness. We treat it like a blemish we need to hide. Personal responsibility, in contrast, provides a set of tools with which to face the problem. Unfortunately when your child is brain-injured, no appropriate instructions arrive as to how to use the set. The less scope you have to take constructive action in a situation central to your family, the more likely you are to conclude that you are to blame for it.

Some sibs understandably looked about for someone else to take responsibility. Remarkably few chose the doctor. God was preferred. God's protagonists usually, although not always, ended up atheists. (Changing one's view of God completely may make the situation more understandable but it means going still further out on a limb when your

182

position is already precarious.) Sibs' reactions to God were also indirect responses to their parents.

A thirteen-year-old declared, 'God is cruel to send me a brother like Jack. I don't go to church now.'

A nine-year-old boy said simply, 'It made me angry with God.'

An eighteen-year-old girl had taken the idea further. 'I cannot believe anybody or anything as powerful as God is supposed to be would let suffering of the innocent occur on a widespread scale.'

Other children were anxious to excuse God but it seemed to me they were sometimes unhappy with their explanations.

'I think God has put these children on earth to teach us a very hard lesson,' said an eight-year-old. 'How lucky we are!'

A boy of thirteen said, 'I wonder how God can be so beastly to make him handicapped, but I suppose it's to show other people how lucky they are.'

You get the feeling the message doesn't ring true. I have noticed that people rarely praise God for their health and the sight of handicap is more often threatening than inspiring. Nevertheless, a family with genuinely optimistic spiritual views offers reassurance. 'I am a Catholic,' a nineteen-year-old girl declared. 'Ken is our angel with the broken wing. We lit a candle for him at Walsingham.'

A little boy said firmly, 'If it weren't for God, Peter would not be here.'

If Ken and Peter are allowed to be people with whom you can get irritated as well as being emblematic of divine forces at work on earth, there is something to be said for this philosophy.

Anne told me, 'When Mark came home my mother said, "Jesus has sent us this baby. Others may react unkindly but don't let this bother you." I wanted to protect him. If I saw another Down's Syndrome child I wanted to hug him.'

It is the openness of children that is the quality sought after by the words: 'Unless you come as little children you shall not reach the Kingdom of Heaven.'

'Philip's special, he's still like a little boy. We were told no matter what he did he'd go straight to Heaven and be a saint soon,' Pam, his grown-up sister, remembered. I asked whether she still believed this about her brother. She laughed.

'I'm not so sure now that he'll be a saint.'

Marie emphasized her Roman Catholic faith. 'It's helped me to see Tom as a gift. I accept all my reactions as part of me. He's there for me to learn from. Tom knows who God is. He's started his first Communion. He loves going to church and he sees Jesus as a friend.'

A mother whose second child was stillborn and whose third, Susie, has spasticity and deafness, explained her own position. 'When I knew I'd lost my baby I cried, "God, I haven't been that wicked!" I lost all conventional faith. Now through Susie I believe there is a purpose in everything that happens. I believe the earth has rules like a mother with her child and if we break them there is chaos.'

In the end it didn't seem to matter whether or not parents had a religious faith or personal spiritual awareness (a number believed in reincarnation) provided there was a positive quality to their thought. This is a lot to ask of ordinary men and women. A kind of wartime spirit has to be generated in your own front room while the rest of the neighbourhood is blissfully unaware that bombs are falling on you. People's potential often rockets in lousy situations and the reality of a brain-injured child is a steady lifetime of battle stations.

Not all sibs suffered from guilt or religious crises but they all had to cope with embarrassment, partly for themselves and partly for their kin. The closer a hurt kid looks to a well one, the more acute the anxiety. There is still the edge of a hope that he will be accepted as normal. While the other children put on their own shoes and get ready to go home, Alex plays on, the urgency escapes him. This is a torture to Garath who can see how such small things emphasize the division between his brother and their mates.

Although many sibs are rich in the knowledge that they have something special to give, finding a role in a large family may be difficult. If you don't have a very definite relationship with the hurt kin round which your family revolves, you are on your way to becoming an outsider.

Ian, who is mentally and physically handicapped, was very naturally a guest at his sister Karen's thirteenth birthday. She worried beforehand, understanding the need for solidarity but already afraid some friends might not come. As they sat down to eat, a young guest burst into tears and left the room without an explanation. The incident cut deeply into Karen. She imagines the pleasures of showing off a well elder brother although she has Neil who is two years older. But Neil is real and Karen is at the age to be going after dreams. She has to be careful not to blame everything on Ian.

What Karen admitted to compared with what she actually endures left room for speculation. She, like so many others, must feel it is only worth being articulate if there are solutions available. Theorizing is no help. She needs a chance to express her own personality without reference to Ian. Hers is a very caring family. Nevertheless she is the only girl and since Ian is managed so well by Neil and tolerated so well by Martin it is hard for her not to feel alone.

All siblings need to have access to someone they trust outside the family who will stand back while they let off steam.

Eighteen-year-old Max has two younger sisters, Alice, sixteen, and Belle, thirteen. Max is sympathetic and personable but having Down's Syndrome means that 'knowing when to stop' can be a social problem. He's very single-minded. He makes you laugh but as a mimic he irritates because he has not learned that the skill of the best comics is not overdoing the joke. Now he's grown tall and strong, his anger is more difficult to contain. He nearly strangled Belle in a friendly wrestling match. Belle seems unperturbed by this ordeal. The family have persuaded Max not to masturbate in public. His sexual awareness both embarrassed and enlightened the two girls. Since you cannot escape from life with your injured kin you must move further into understanding it. Belle longs for her mother's time. While we talk she climbs onto her lap and buries her face. Max is Max. 'It's nice to be on holiday without him but we miss him and want him back,' says Alice.

Belle remembers the time Max put the dog in the oven, so the dog had to go. Their father, fearful of arriving home to find a family pet baked, decreed 'No more dogs.'

'We thought we were heartbroken,' Alice said, 'but we got over it.'

There are always contradictions because family loyalty is strong. The truth is a mixture of things and this is hard for sibs to get across. They are aware that some people might come away thinking either 'Handicapped kids like that should be in institutions' or 'They seem to manage very well, I don't see that they need my help (or understanding or consideration).'

Max's eccentricity doesn't always cause embarrassment. During Alice's birthday party at a restaurant he emerged from the toilets beaming with his trousers round his ankles. 'No one noticed,' their mother explains. 'He got them up in the end and had the whole dining room singing Happy Birthday . . .'

Alice says, 'He still believes in Father Christmas. Opening presents is magic for him. The snooker table he had last year was ruined in a day but it was worth it because he had so much fun.'

The father of a twelve-year-old autistic boy called Jonathan explained that he never knew whether to be embarrassed or to laugh. 'There's something so honest about Jonathan's behaviour. For instance, he walked up to a model in the British Home Stores and shook hands with it. The arm came off and when he tried to put it back the head fell off so he tucked the lot under his arm and gave them to his brother . . .'

Jonathan's fifteen-year-old brother Philip agrees: 'He has a habit of disappearing into the Ladies, especially when I'm with him, and I have to tiptoe in to get him out.'

Jonathan is always included. Philip says, 'We accept that he's likely to stand on the table in the café and demand a drink. There was the time we were all in a Chinese restaurant and Jonathan put his arm in the fish tank . . .'

With the best will in the world, once you are out with an unconventional child things will tend to liven up.

Philip underlines the ambiguity of a sib's position: 'I have to keep an eye on my brother all the time. It doesn't give me much freedom. At the same time, I don't feel I've lost much.'

Talking was always a relief to sibs. I began to realize that due to years of holding back they had become remarkably good at disguising their feelings.

Fourteen-year-old Gavin spoke about his seventeen-year-old brother Mike. At first I was only made aware of the seizures (with which Gavin thought himself adequate to cope). Later it was pointed out to me that Mike had major physical problems. Gavin remembers, 'By the time I was about five I thought Mike'd get better and I kept asking when. At about eight or nine I realized it wouldn't happen. I was angry for him but I didn't tell anyone because somehow I thought they'd laugh. I would've liked a friend to talk to then.'

There are problems when your only brother or sister has a severe disability. Sibs need guts. There's not going to be a hope in hell that your kin will be passed off as normal or nearly normal when the wheelchair appears and other kids look in.

You have to have self-confidence. Gavin felt Mike could command a little more dignity if he didn't make so much noise when he was pushed along. Of course he knows that Mike is just trying his best to communicate but most people can't cope with the spectacle. When they want to defy the gods, Gavin pushes Mike very fast indeed.

The likelihood of the entire family being cut off from normal social life depends on the degree of injury and the amount of time taken up in the sheer physical management of a household with a child with special needs. Finding the right balance is often almost impossible without realistic outside support. And you are already aware that the problem is unlikely to decrease with age.

Jenny talks of her brother David: 'I take issue with all those who say Down's Syndrome people are such happy people. My brother is intelligent enough to realize he is not normal, and yet he cannot really understand his condition. He has suffered endless frustration wondering why he can't do the things my sister and I can do. Why can't he learn to drive? Is he going to marry, go to university, have a house of his own? He knows when he looks in the mirror that his face is different and at one point he wouldn't look in the mirror. I am fond of him and his unhappiness hurts me.'

As sibs get older still, a new anxiety appears. The consciousness that their parents won't live for ever impinges on their thoughts.

Jack was born when his autistic brother was three. Twenty years later his parents asked him how he would cope if they died.

'I really wouldn't like to be put in that position – but think I can live with it. I'd resent it if I were left with Steven cold or if Ben, my younger brother, were not around or if the responsibility had come at an earlier time. It could have been a really tough job. But he has come far enough so that he wouldn't be *that* much of a burden.'

A group of grown-up siblings met to discuss their memories of discomfiting stares and other innocent cruelties. Some recalled the numbers of social events, parties and weddings they were forced to miss because their handicapped brothers or sisters couldn't go. Others felt neglected by their preoccupied parents or feared that their own children might be born retarded, but the predominant anxiety was the talk of promises to care for their hurt kin for the rest of their lives. With this came the question: 'What do you tell your boyfriend or girlfriend? How are you going to incorporate your future husband or wife into your problems?' Such fears can haunt sibs from early adolescence onwards.

The sibs' position is tortuous. There is a powerful sibling tie, a feeling of responsibility and in most cases very deep affection. This has to be measured against the unremitting loss of liberty and friendship imposed on a sib who will constantly have to favour her kin's interests before her own.

Spending one's childhood in this way is one thing, the rest of one's life is another matter.

A fifteen-year-old girl wrote: 'I like looking after him if he doesn't drive me mad. But I think he will . . .' She can see the trap and she's frightened.

A fourteen-year-old boy said: 'It's okay looking after him now as he is my friend – but if I want to do something else I get annoyed.'

This is not unreasonable. When school finishes, who is going to be there as translator, comrade, body servant, while one's mother does the washing, changes the baby, cooks the dinner and so forth?

Perhaps you share the domestic chores. You know how

hard your mother works, with what good spirit. You admire her. You do want to help her. But few sibs actually fancy being *like* her for the rest of their own lives. A twelve-year-old girl with an autistic brother of eighteen wrote desperately, 'I don't really want to look after him because he will take up a lot of my time and patience and anyway I don't much like him.'

The business of 'not liking' him, however, is insufficiently powerful to erase him from the memory.

Marie's fifteen-year-old brother Tom now lives in a hostel down the road. Her mother has a chronic illness requiring constant hospitalization. The accommodation is a good compromise because the place is very near but Marie expresses a lingering sadness that this is how things are. All children grow up and most leave home. We look upon it as their decision. This is very different from sending your child into residential care, because even though it may ultimately be for the best you know it was not his choice. Tom's mother feels inadequate when other parents tell her, 'Oh, I'd never put my child away.' 'We live in a hilly area,' says Marie, 'and the hostel is at the bottom. Going back is painful for Mum but she still does it nearly every day. He comes home every other weekend and sometimes Mum brings him home for a treat or just for love. If I'm home I'll go down to the hostel and give him a bath. He still sees me as more of a playmate. He gives me lots of kisses. But with Tom you feel things should last for ever. It's not that he doesn't want to grow up, it's that he doesn't understand it.' Marie's life goes on. 'I'm leaving for university next term and I realize Tom won't know where I'm going or why I've gone. It hurts me deeply because I can't explain. I'm afraid Tom will think I've rejected him. The separation reminds me of him not understanding when the children mocked him and I find I'm going through all that grief again. My mother has always said that she doesn't want me to feel that I have to be responsible . . .'

Because there is no acknowledgement of what sibs achieve while they are young, there is no graduation. You just go on doing as much as you can for as long as you can. You continue to think about what you could have done or might do for the rest of your life.

I heard of families who shut their doors to lick their unhealable wounds. This isn't an extraordinary reaction. If you don't want to be pitied or humiliated, if you can't bear being told 'It's all right' when it patently isn't, if you can't stand keeping up a pretence that you're all fine, or that your old friends aren't making excuses for not coming round, then it is easier to slam the door on a hostile world. Inside, you can at least be real. The contradiction arises that by doing this you foster more ignorance and prejudice. If everyone who was left-handed or blue-eyed stayed indoors and refused to mix socially, people with these characteristics would soon become very sinister indeed.

One father asked me to point out that TV and radio had gone so over the top on the subject of handicap that no one wanted to know about individual opinions. 'People think everything is being taken care of,' he said. 'It's hard to convince them we're still handicapped – the whole family, that is. We simply can't drop everything and rush off somewhere. We can't be spontaneous, everything has to be planned.'

Some people may assume that everything necessary is being done for families with a handicapped child. Others may feel that their own difficulties are enough and no further responsibilities can be taken on board. There is also a remarkable ignorance of what is needed and what one could do to improve matters. Sibs' darkest moments are those of isolation and misunderstanding; they need the confidence that they can share their experience with those who are outside it.

CHAPTER 12

The Politics of Handicap

What is being done and what else could be done? Why has a more significant response to the situation not developed? Right from the beginning many families I spoke to were unaware whether or not they were supposed to have a social worker. Certainly no one knew why they had or hadn't a social worker. When I enquired into this mystery I discovered that the business of linking a social worker with a family is entirely dependent upon the hospital consultant or GP identifying the needs. Social workers are known to go scouting the wards hunting for trade but if the consultant doesn't believe in referring cases to them, they can't argue. The situation varies enormously around the country. One of the consultants at our nearest big hospital prefers not to involve social workers. He breaks the news to parents, then disappears to leave the necessary comforting to the nursing staff. These professionals, however wonderful, cannot provide the all-important continuity between the hospital and the home, nor do they have enough information about the various kinds of help that parents are going to need.

Social workers exist because no other field makes people's feelings a primary concern. If medical and nursing teams are to assume even part of the responsibility for giving emotional support, they need to study the needs of their clients.

Paediatricians and obstetricians are used to dealing with 'The Normal Child'. Abnormality represents a kind of failure for them, especially if there's not much they can do about it. After treating a brain-injured child for a new complaint that seems to be curable, they will give it back to its mother smiling, 'Well, that fixes her/him up.' This is done with such sleight of hand that the mother has no time to point out the fact that the child in question is still blind, deaf, dumb and paralysed. The physicians do not enquire about the rest of the family largely because they do not wish to know. The omnipotent consultant who has just treated a broken limb successfully hardly wants it pointed out that, with massive neurological problems, the child is not ever likely to walk. Thus he forgets the owner of the limb and her family and only remembers that he pinned it well and that it mended beautifully. I was told of a midwife who on delivering an infant with a hair lip and cleft palate exclaimed, 'Oh, what a beautiful baby girl.' She could have said, 'She's a fine healthy baby – but she doesn't look too pretty at this moment.' The words 'It'll be all right' ring in the ears of parents who know only too well that the situation is wildly wrong. They want to have the evidence of their own eyes acknowledged so that they might justifiably ask what is to be done.

Social workers are used to dealing with unusual situations but their traditional focus is the mother-child relationship rather than sibling to sibling. This overlooks both the problems and the potential in the rest of the household. It puts the children's relationships with each other effectively 'below stairs'. Listening to siblings with respect makes the matter initially more complicated but it also resolves many difficulties quickly, as well as bringing to light experiences that need to be recognized.

The case loads of most social workers are ludicrously

high, often into the hundreds. What possible kind of individual concern *can* you give anyone if your visits are weeks, sometimes months apart? Despite these factors it remains in a social worker's power to help siblings feel more appreciated and less isolated.

In theory siblings have access to local schools and could go there to talk about issues involved. Teachers are frequently unaware that the preoccupied child who always hands in his homework late is actually doing two jobs. It is illegal for children to accept paid work that interferes with their study. Unpaid work is another matter. But if the mother were a single parent or the family unemployed and the sibs *had* been paid, the sum would probably be deducted from their social security benefit or the family income supplement.

June, a single parent, who struggles courageously for her daughter Joleyn's rehabilitation, manages to earn the £4 a week maximum extra allowed by the DHSS. She lives just outside the mileage limitation for a school taxi so she worked a little harder to cover its price. When she informed the DHSS, her benefit was neatly cut to cancel out her efforts – she had to go on pushing Joleyn to school.

Since this is the normal state of affairs under our present system, I phoned up our local branch of the DHSS. I was put through to a very charming woman who, as is their present policy, preferred to remain anonymous. They say that this is because their staff move about so much between departments, which is somewhat implausible. The ruling seems to exist to protect officers from unhappy clients. At any rate, they have created a faceless body worthy of the most spirited characterization of totalitarian government. However pleasant the disembodied female voice on the line, without access to a name, once the receiver was down I had no evidence that she had ever existed. It is very hard to have an argument or even to beg or plead with someone who won't admit to actually being there.

A mother hopes for some miserable addition to her benefit for heating or clothing her handicapped child. She phones and writes but she never knows to whom she is talking or whether her arguments are fairly considered. The letters back are signed with an illegible cipher. DHSS rules are exceedingly complex, often needing a lawyer to unravel them. There is a code which interprets these rules but this is kept at DHSS regional offices and is not available to the members of the public unless they have the time and money to go there. It is unlikely that a single parent with three children, one in a wheelchair, is going to make the journey very easily even if she knew that the code book existed – I do not hear of the information being widely advertised! However, the anonymous lady to whom I spoke did seem genuinely sympathetic.

'It is hard for single parents with a handicapped child,' she said. 'They can get passed from one department to another because they don't fit into any category. They do sometimes have to wait a long time but it's only because we're trying to do our best for them.'

Unfortunately, if you haven't enough fuel or the price of a taxi to take your spastic daughter to school you can't afford to wait. If you earn the money you're penalized. The state would apparently sooner see your kids were adequately fed in care than allow you to provide for them in your home. The single parent family with its handicapped member is almost commonplace, so why is there no DHSS category for them?

On this question of handicap the DHSS lady sighed. 'Yes, benefit officers are often saddened that they can't do more. We can't even give the single payments for clothing, a special pair of shoes for instance, that we could three

months ago. As to the difficulties of part-time earnings,'
she sighed again, 'we do like our clients to move straight
into full-time occupation.'

'But a mother with a disabled kid can't be expected to
do that,' I said.

'That's very unfortunate. We do have to obey the
rules.'

'What do you expect people to do?'

'It's difficult,' she said, 'very difficult. However, the earnings allowance is due to be reviewed in April 1988. We are
expecting changes. I can't tell you anything yet . . .'

Perhaps some day you won't be a criminal for trying to
supply your athetoid son with a pair of boots.

There should be some spin-off in all this for siblings.
Their parents' morale is of immense importance to them. I
do not think government is yet awakened either to their
need or to their contribution.

An educational psychologist remarked to me, 'I sometimes notice that the child who opens the door is looking
as though she hoped I'd come for her too.' You cannot
extract disabled children from their families, assess them
and then put them back. The whole family experiences the
handicap always, always, always . . .

I talked to my friend Magda Szlenkier who has worked
for years with Contact a Family, an organization founded
to develop a community work approach for families with
handicapped children in Wandsworth, South London. CAF
are unusual because they include children with every type
of disability plus their siblings and fathers. One of the
mothers summed up her involvement: 'They've got parents
together. A lot of us felt very guilty and it's helped us to
talk and shake us out of it.'

Another mother explained, 'If we hadn't been with them
we'd never have got out. Public transport is too difficult.

With the group, no one is ever embarrassed. If you have an accident, they always find some way round it.'

When a mother can't manage a wheelchair with her hurt child, it's unlikely she'll cope with young sibs hanging on by the side. The whole family are restricted in their movements unless there is help to hand. I could see that the help CAF were giving was improving the quality of the siblings' lives, and of the hurt child's.

'Rita's gone places she wouldn't have otherwise. She's got lots of local friends. She's at a special school covering a wide area – she had no local friends before.'

When a sib can see her handicapped brother is getting the chance to have fun she's more likely to go ahead and enjoy herself without being lumbered by guilt. Moreover, sibs can feel rather proud that their kin has some kind of independent life which increases their credibility in the eyes of the world.

'Amy lives for the swimming club and all the discos – they're fun things for her.'

The co-ordinators of CAF are quite well aware of the emotional difficulties parents have to overcome. Once a mother commits the family to joining, she knows she has publicly acknowledged that her child has a disability. You cannot of course deal with a problem until you've admitted to it but all of us at some stage find this hard.

'The first meeting was too overpowering. There were a lot of people and a lot of handicapped children. It horrified me. I suddenly realized what having a handicapped child was going to be like in the future. After that the co-ordinator would often phone. Despite my rejecting her several times, she'd keep gently encouraging me to come along. Finally I did go to a coffee morning. I really loved it and the people I met.'

Stephanie is divorced and has three children. The

youngest, Andrew, is mentally handicapped and suffers from epileptic fits, usually once a day or more. He has no speech and his frustration can be disruptive. Andrew is now ten but Stephanie first took him to a CAF event when he was three.

'I saw all these grown-up handicapped kids. I hadn't visualized Andrew – my golden-haired little moppet – being an adult. It was quite startling – a bigger shock than the first initial idea that there was something wrong with him anyway . . . There was a time for about two years when I went every week. It was my day out, believe it or not. I didn't have any method of transport and I didn't know anybody, my life was confined to the local shops . . . My little girl Diana had a lot of enjoyment. She was the real reason we started with CAF. It was lovely the things that were being done and the attention for the brothers and sisters. Other charities arrange outings for your handicapped child but the whole family is often overlooked.'

So CAF gives the social support that is so essential. After all, humankind *is* a social animal and if the balance goes wrong we suffer. A high percentage of members gave as one of their reasons for joining CAF the help it offered sibs.

Noreen Miller who initiated and developed CAF has humour and receptivity blended with her crusading spirit. When she sees a need, she acts on it. This is refreshing in an area where problems are urgent and red tape clogs so many lives.

Handicapped children need to be integrated from the playgroup onwards. No matter what their disabilities, as soon as hurt and well kids join forces, understanding and caring are developed both in the young and *by* the young. Small children can be very perceptive. When they realize that someone actually needs help they are usually pleased and proud to give it.

'Unfortunately,' says Magda, 'society rewards the wrong achievements too highly. We are very keen on a socially imposed good self-image. Disability is seen as a negative thing and many parents don't want their children contaminated by it. It is possible to change attitudes. If the playgroups were there and publicized, mothers and fathers might be encouraged to take their children along and find out.'

She told me about a remarkable family. 'They were working class, six kids. The eight-year-old was mentally handicapped. They had a policy of treating the children absolutely the same. All the kids joined in, they were unvaryingly caring towards the others and the eight-year-old was extremely secure and communicative – you'd forget his handicap. On the other hand,' she went on, 'I've seen sibs pushed into the background by everyone. While the mother is fighting to cope, the social services don't take much notice. She or her children usually have to have passed breaking point and by then it's inevitably too late. Another eight-year-old boy had to go into a special unit because he was pretending to be handicapped – copying his brother's behaviour. He stayed there until he was fifteen. Social workers should look into the dynamics of the whole family. The closer the age gap, the more problems are likely. Sibs' positions must be seen and felt as positive, that's why CAF makes sibs participants.'

'What about social workers?' I asked. 'All the other professionals I've talked to delegate responsibility for sibs onto them.'

'Unfortunately social workers aren't encouraged to show their *own* feelings. Ideally they should be sufficiently secure to be able to express personal emotions without overimposing them. Our families need the support of warm relationships. If they suspect their social worker is acting out a role they clam up. If you want to be trusted you have to be yourself. Kids always work on an intuitive level — they see immediately when you're not real.'

Magda pointed to the advantages of family counselling coming from health visitors.

'Many people still view the appearance of the social worker as a stigma. That's the person who arrives when your husband is on the booze and your daughter steals from Woolworth's.'

Health visitors work with all children up to the age of five. Magda wanted the provision of specialist health visitors who could be asked to join a family from the moment of diagnosis. She could also see a need for co-counselling. Immediate links with other parents and sibs means initial anger and grief can be shared.

'Nobody wants to be told "It's all right" when they feel they are the only ones in the world to whom this has happened.'

Brain injury and birth handicap are as surrounded by euphemisms and platitudes as death itself. But you are not burying your child. She or he is already changing your life and the lives of your other children and you need to know what to do about it.

While I was sitting in the offices of CAF a name and number were thrust into my hand. 'Try Pauline Fairbrother at Mencap,' they said. 'She edits *Sibs*, the news sheet for siblings. It's a pioneering venture.'

Pauline was possibly just old enough to be my mother but she looked so young and her energy and enthusiasm ran alongside a dry wit born of years of being indefatigable.

'I once spoke to over twenty ESN schools on the subject of sibs,' she said. 'Nothing came back but you can't stop just because some people won't listen. You've got to learn to put it another way. It'd be so easy to give up, wouldn't it? I don't like to be that easy.'

'I just wish,' wrote one reader of Pauline's news sheet, 'that as the sister of a fifteen-year-old mentally handicapped young madam I'd known about *Sibs* many years ago. So often one feels *so* alone, as if you're the only person alive in such a position. I'm sure many people find great relief from isolation via your group.'

Sibs is campaigning. 'What we are suggesting,' Pauline said, 'is that children should be invited during school hours to their handicapped brother's or sister's school. Once there they can be helped to understand the nature of the various handicaps and their sibling's education. They can share anxieties, resentments, love and joys.'

The newsletter discusses the way successful support groups for sibs have been set up in the USA and New Zealand. The children's ages ranged from five to twelve and they were delighted to comment.

'Let's think what it would be like to be your brother or sister.'

'You know what to do if someone pulls a face at them.'

'I know how to handle her when she throws a wobbly.'

Pauline says: 'The hardest task is convincing parents and professionals that there is any problem at all. Just being aware is enough to start with. Every family with a mentally handicapped child should be given counselling and support. How we help these children depends on the customs of the society in which they live, on how families see themselves and on what is acceptable and what is not. In developing countries, families remain physically and emotionally close all their lives. What is expected and usually accepted happily by brothers and sisters is an unquestioning responsibility for each other. Their families are usually larger and embrace more relationships than just one set of parents and children.'

I was reminded of a Third World scheme called 'Child to Child'. Its object is to teach older children about health care, including how to detect and assist with handicap. Their job is then to pass this information down to the younger ones. Our schools offer little information about the practical help children can give to children. Because the context is different we underestimate the child. What is precious about childhood is that one enjoys learning, which is not the same thing as being taught. The process is best when kids hear ideas that excite them from other kids.

One of the difficulties encountered in setting up sibling groups was that some children were less than happy to be labelled as 'having a problem'. Perhaps it would be an idea to approach sibs as people who are attempting to find solutions. To be told that what you are doing is so worthwhile it merits support from the outside is a rather different proposition and can't possibly make you feel like a case history. It should be recognized by now that siblings themselves represent a worldwide charity without a title.

Another way of helping sibs might have occurred to you. It is by actively involving them in a programme of work designed to get their hurt kin better. A long intensive daily regime is unrealistic for most families. But looking at what the Kerland Foundation has achieved over a short period of time encourages me to imagine that many sibs would thrive simply because their hurt brother or sister *had* a three-hour daily programme. If I examine the benefits, the disadvantages will perhaps appear less as deterrents and more as obstacles we can find ways to overcome . . .

Sibs do suffer because we do not expect anyone handicapped to get well. When the gang sees the boy in the wheelchair has a broken leg they don't mock the girl who's pushing him. A broken leg may be painful and involve tedious visits to hospital but it inspires good humour on the part of all concerned. This is partly because everyone knows pretty clearly what the matter is and that the bright and cheerful victim is expected to recover. A potentially curable condition, even if there are risks attached to it, encourages people to feel hopeful and positive about what medical science and individual determination can achieve. We're all eager to write our names on the plaster of Paris. We're relieved that it doesn't belong to us but we can identify with the situation. If it happened to us we think we could cope.

Should the wheelchair contain a thin twisted heap drooling at the mouth, our expression changes. We are convinced that no cure is possible. Added to that, there seems to be little evidence that this near-corpse is sufficiently conscious of the predicament to fight for recovery. Should we inadvertently notice a flicker of inner spirit in such a face we shudder and forget. 'At least,' we like to console ourselves, 'they don't understand.' We cannot identify with the uncomprehending eyes or the deformed body. We maintain privately that it couldn't have happened to us because *we* would rather be dead. *We* wouldn't hang obstinately on to life, a burden to everyone. Not to have been born would be best; otherwise death is the decent thing. This line of thought allows the apparition pushed by a doting sister to be justifiably distasteful. We resent it. Likewise we resent the girl who makes us feel guilty by presenting her brother thus unashamedly to the world. When the gang starts jeering 'Your brother's off his rocker', we are rather relieved that everybody feels the same because it makes us less beastly. If we are ten years old perhaps we join in.

This is an extreme way of putting it. Even if we have conquered many of these feelings, the residual unease remains. It always does when we are helpless in the face of suffering. If news gets around that something can be done (as it did with cancer), some of the deathliness, the fear and the guilt begin to melt away. The fact that a sibling has a sister whom half the neighbourhood thinks it worth helping puts an entirely different perspective on the whole matter. Also your hurt kin doesn't just sit around, she works. Somehow or another, despite the eccentricities involved, this creates a more normal situation than living with the constant knowledge that nothing can be done. It seems less than natural to accept disability passively. It is also impossible if you are to survive at all.

Most families fight all the time to do something. Their dilemma is never knowing precisely what is best or for how long or in what order. It is easy to be caught up by the diverse and disruptive symptoms of the injury. By trying to encourage your child to speak or straighten his legs or not throw food about, you forget that the root of the trouble is actually in his brain. It is a considerable relief to stop speculating about the endless variety of different problems likely to occur in a day, a week, a lifetime of handicap, and get on with the practical business of rehabilitating that brain so that its owner can walk and talk, think and tie shoe laces. Suddenly a sib can describe her brother's problem and what is being done for it. Nothing succeeds like success. You boast to the kids down the road: 'My sister can crawl two hundred feet.'

A small boy whose handicapped elder sister had always been an individual set apart joyfully discovers she's learned all about dinosaurs. He rushes off to school to announce, 'My sister's on a programme and now knows *everything* about dinosaurs.' His comrades are suitably impressed. Every week he's asked, 'What else does your sister know?'

The structure of The Kerland Foundation's three-hour programme which aims at best to rehabilitate your child and place her or him back into mainline education changes the outlook for an entire family. No one need feel that their hurt kin isn't being fully helped. At the same time, having given her that daily three hours, there is the huge relief that once it's over you can have normal family priorities.

This was Kathy Boston's reaction: 'The structure has the benefit of allowing me to switch off from Jessica once the programme is over and give a hundred per cent of my attention to the others instead of only fifty per cent attention all the time because of a constant worry that Jessica was just sitting there.' Jessica's siblings are Elizabeth, her twin, who is just five, Christopher who is seven, and Holly, ten. 'The older children are content to do homework or watch TV while I'm programming; occasionally they help. I don't push them one way or the other. They will, however, show her toys or read to her which I think is a terrific contribution.'

Even having a well baby and a hurt toddler can seem better when you have a clear programme of work that you feel is pulling your injured child free of his problem.

The baby here is called Holly, her brother on the programme is Simon.

'Coping with Holly proved to be easier than I had anticipated, although at first my days were much more tiring, I was on the go all the time. Mornings were worst, getting the children ready by 10 a.m. when Holly was sometimes taking as much as an hour over her feeds. But as time has gone by I'm convinced that Simon being on a programme has made life easier for all of us. Our days have a structure and a purpose.' And Holly enjoys the convivial atmosphere. 'She's very sociable and there's no doubt she'd be a bored little girl without all the activity that goes with having a brain-injured child on programme.'

The patterners who come to the house bringing children, toys, even animals, in their wake create an unbeatably positive current between your household and the outside world. They become your new extended family. You are no longer isolated, there are friends to fight on your behalf. Their unusual intimacy with the situation makes them uniquely able to predict your needs, and to respect your children.

The objective is not, of course, undertaken lightly. Claire writes: 'I knew that both the twelve hours a day and the six hours a day programme would be impossible for me to sustain. I have a five-year-old daughter Jennifer and one-year-old twins, besides my little Victoria who has Down's Syndrome. I heard about the Kerland Foundation's five-day-week, three hours a day programme which seemed much more realistic so we paid them a visit. I felt that if I was to succeed then I couldn't and wouldn't risk my relationship with Jennifer.'

Victoria's mother manages to do nearly all the sessions while Jennifer is at school.

'To date she is accepting the situation extremely well. She seems to want this work to help Victoria. I have allocated other types of stimulation especially for her to give Victoria because she really likes to be involved.' Occasionally the programme has to be done out of school hours but 'Jennifer is happy to play with the patterners' children and it's surprising how quickly time can pass.'

The general agreement is that a structure and a programme that is having a very positive effect are actually both emotionally and physically liberating.

'The very strict routine which I find necessary during the week has ironically helped me to cope with all the family demands, and for the first time since Victoria was born I actually feel as though I get a proper weekend.'

Another advantage of Kerland for sibs is that they are linked into it. They know the other families on programme, either through personal contact when they congregate for a potentially riotous weekend at a hotel in Kidderminster, or through the newsletter. They are proud and delighted to see their efforts as fund-raisers in newspaper headlines.

As matters stand, of course, even a three-hour daily programme would prove very difficult if not impossible for many families. One answer is much more sympathetic back-up from the Social Services and schools. Some, although by no means all, families on programme are 'punished' for their initiative by the disapproval of their doctors and the non-cooperation of health visitors, teachers, and physios. This can be particularly upsetting for young single parents who have to be very brave to cope with uninformed prejudice when they need understanding and (at least) moral support. At the time of writing these last chapters, I heard that the Kerland Foundation was closing down. Soon I shall be relying on my own less usual experience of motherhood, late-night perusal of back copies of the *New Scientist*, and my home-grown appetite for questioning the established order of things to help my children spread their wings as they relish the gift of life.

The evolving relationship between Lili and Doran has allowed me to recognise that there is an emotional dynamic to the recovery process to which siblings richly but often unwittingly contribute. The challenged child studies her sibling closely and weighs up what can be copied, fought over, shared, or sympathised with. For their part, siblings oversee fair play, and when challenged kin reap the benefits of a daily developmental programme on which they are obliged to work, they cease to appear as idealised angels and become ordinary children leading extraordinary lives. At which point, everybody benefits.

CHAPTER 13

———◆◆◆———

Recognition and Change

'In my end is my beginning.' In this chapter I want to review some of the factors I have left out, re-emphasize those things you have already heard and paint a picture of how sibs could best be served by all of us.

When you first talk to the other children you don't know whether to suggest that they are ready to take a degree on the subject of handicap or assume that they already have one. They can tell you enormous amounts about conventional drugs and their effects. They know about preparing food and the best ways to get it into kids who are hard to feed. They can take off callipers and surgical boots and put on spinal jackets and large nappies. They are skilled in calling the doctor at appropriate times and they can motivate or pacify when the occasion demands. It is true that the more you do, the less time you have to sit down and think, 'What about me? What's to become of me?' Getting on with the job is a challenge and those who can and do get on with it are certainly better off than those who are still desperately pretending it hasn't happened.

Graham is nearly seven. His elder sister and younger brother are both brain-injured. When I met him he was set on being a doctor. He rattled off all the bones in the body at enormous speed and then began on the respiratory system. His teachers remark that unlike the other children he always wants to stay and talk.

'Is it the aorta that carries the blood, Mum?' he asks. 'I want to explain the circulatory system to Linda. I want to make every handicapped child well and give them all toys.'

The information that sibs pick up shows the degree of their receptivity. Yet there are no schemes to inform them.

The story of Andrew's teeth illustrates the gulf between the family and the doctors.

'Andrew loves sweets,' Sue said. 'He can eat them all day so he's always had bad teeth. Last year he went into hospital to have them filled and when he was coming round afterwards Mum saw they'd taken every one out. They'd never told us and they weren't going to give him false ones because they were afraid he'd swallow them. My mum was in tears.'

Personally, I've always been terrified of losing *any* teeth and the look of pure horror that passed over my face assured Sue of my feelings.

'It turned out all right though,' she said, unexpectedly smiling.

'They gave him dentures?'

'No, his gums got so hard he could still chew his sweets. Mum had been worried that Andrew wouldn't be able to enjoy the toffee.'

At this point I didn't know whether to laugh or to cry. You may do both. There is a contrast between this loving family's intimate understanding of what gives Andrew pleasure and the impersonal hospital surgeon who failed to communicate his intentions.

Andrew's consultant was occupied with the sheer mechanics of the problem. Bad teeth are better out. How loss of teeth could affect the life of a mentally handicapped youth and his family were below his level of concern. That is worth crying over. Ah, but the happy ending is the restoration of Andrew's ability to crunch confectionery without teeth. It is touching that his family put his pleasure before even his teeth but wouldn't it have been better the other way round? Did no one suggest that too much sugar is bad for any kid, and that in brain-injured kids who have far less ability to get rid of toxins the effect could be disastrous? If Sue had been taught all this by a health visitor while she was still a child, think of the pleasure she would have taken in passing on the information. One of the prodigious benefits of the Kerland Foundation is that they do care about diet. They understand that a toxic brain is not going to be a well-functioning one, that food full of the right vitamins and so on makes you better motivated and generally happier because it creates health. The finer their comprehension of the issues surrounding their kin, the more sibs like it. They are keen to act but don't always know how to begin.

Frances is sixteen. 'Because Paul has Down's,' she says, 'I've learned to understand what people like him need. I'd like to do something to help, raise money, anything, but they say I'm too young. When I try to explain my ideas I feel they just think, "Oh, she's not old enough to know." It's very frustrating.'

Recognition cannot be emphasized enough.

I remember when a TV news team came down to film Doran. The tiny cottage was bursting with equipment and technicians. Everyone was fascinated by Doran's curiosity and self-assurance. They ignored Lili. Her early enthusiasm completely deflated, she disappeared quietly upstairs.

'Look,' I said, 'the happiness we've all enjoyed has been largely due to my daughter, but none of you seems to have noticed her.'

The wand was waved, and in five minutes Lili was in front of the cameras, glowing and talking.

'Your daughter's a natural,' they said, surprised and by now very interested. 'How does she know so much? Can she do a bit more? She's been telling us about Doran's girlfriends.' They dashed back to Lili as if she were a unique find that might suddenly fly away.

You will have remembered how many times sibs wished they could stand up in school to talk. No one I interviewed or corresponded with had managed to achieve this miracle. This is surprising because if these children's needs are to be understood, their work must be recognized by their teachers and shared by their fellow pupils. Many of them have brothers or sisters at special schools. Are sibs' teachers aware that this is always a subject for unpleasant playground jokes? There is no chance to defend or explain matters during the rowdiness of break time, so the sib must sink his feelings yet again.

The day the hurt kid in the family is sent to a special school means a division in the household hard for both children and parents to accept.

Garath's mother said: 'I deeply resent the artificial splitting up of my family because of the two schools. I feel it most that Alex can't go to Garath's comprehensive school.'

Pauline Fairbrother's endeavours to create opportunities for the sibs of children in special education to go and share what's happening in their brothers' and sisters' schools are extremely wise. It is equally vital that all children in special education have the chance to spend some time in normal schools. Not just occasionally as a token gesture but regularly as part of a structured programme.

Integration is necessary from the playgroup upwards. Kids should be stimulated to view caring not as an imposition but as the recognition of a natural impulse which they can cultivate. Children are generally encouraged by their curriculum to think but not to feel. Thinking itself is governed by kids' expectations of exam results rather than an individual reflection of their experience.

Our feelings give us a sense of centre. Paying attention

to what kids are *trying* to say is more important than having them feed us what they think we want. The more time children are given to involve themselves in doing something that commends their real abilities to give, the more they feel filled up as human beings.

The prisoners who have raised money for Doran explained that they were never told how good it could feel to help someone else.

'The more I give,' says Shakespeare's Juliet, 'the more I have to give' and she's absolutely right. The theory isn't enough. It's the opportunity that matters. The earlier one has it, the better.

One object of education should be to discover what is most essential for all children so that they are happy to be alive and to find themselves a part of the world in which they are growing up. The energy with which a hurt child fights for full membership of humanity is inspiring. A popular image of handicap is the child who despite disablement believes that life is worth living. Does she offer a picture of hope to the rest of us or do we assume she is merely deluded? A third comment might be that from her very immediate point of view, life looks as though it could be worth living and she intends to contribute. This attitude might be an asset to her more normal peers.

If integration is to be realistic then we need to examine and integrate the philosophies of specialist and normal schools so that all the theoretical advantages can take effect in fact. And it must be realized that those who have the best first-hand experience of integration are sibs. They invariably hold a higher expectation of their brothers and sisters than anyone else. The greater the understanding we have of their home life, the better equipped we are going to be to provide successful integration.

If you are physically handicapped, being at school shouldn't put a new restriction on your mobility. You must resist being kept in your wheelchair for convenience if you can get out of it. The school should be at pains to allow you to move under your own steam. Sitting in a wheelchair is neither physically nor neurologically healthy. It's also boring. All little kids pester parents with 'Let me do it myself'. It is often easier and quicker if the parent takes over, but it's far less useful to the child. A child in a wheelchair does not learn to enjoy that impulse. The chair is cultural. It exists mainly to satisfy our convenience, and the seated position looks more normal and is therefore acceptable. Some years ago hospitals recognized that keeping patients in bed after an operation actually retarded their recovery. By the same logic the longer a child remains in a wheelchair, the more problems she will compound to ensure that she stays there. There are children with severe enough problems to confine them to chairs but with everyone's help many kids could spend more time learning how to move independently on the floor.

The child in the chair learns to depend on it. Throwing him out is often pictured as the worst thing that could happen to him. But arriving on the floor gives him a measure of equality his peers respect. However restricted his mobility, he becomes an initiator. He ceases to be passive. Everything is relative. We happen to be a table and chair culture which makes the division more noticeable.

As normal children learn about the ones who appear to have problems, they also find out about themselves. This has happened to many sibs.

Toby was among the first of the younger sibs I spoke to, and I thought him remarkable. His mother says frankly: 'He has to gain because he's got to cope with the intensity of the psychological problem of his parents. He has to reach a stage when he can analyse himself more deeply and reach a higher level of consciousness than his peers or he will lose.' Gradually I realized Toby was not alone.

213

These 'other' children have a good deal to enjoy from one another's company. Much as they need to be respected for what they actually do, they also require holidays away from it all. So far as I know there are no schemes to send them on holiday together. The freedom to discover who you are away from the dominating influence of your family situation must be highly desirable.

The heroines and heroes of Victorian literature lived lives fraught with moral and ethical dilemmas. Modern writers are more concerned to have characters satisfy their individual needs, and in consequence something has been lost. To enjoy moral and ethical dilemmas you must first care about how your actions affect other people, and vice versa. All sibs are in the thick of this. I do not think the issues raised are easily resolvable or ever could be. Nevertheless, there is more hope for the human condition if we can reach outside ourselves. Confusion is as much part of learning as understanding is. Socrates pointed out that 'the only thing that is obvious is that nothing is obvious'.

Many children suffer severe or profound disabilities. Who they are, how and why they remain alive, are often questions that only the closest members of the family can answer. A mother has the potential for a deep intuitive rapport with her baby, little of which is easily recognized by an outsider. In the case of an injured child, sometimes hardly more than comatose, the intuitive rapport doesn't fade with age.

While children, sibs also cultivate intuitive capacities. Sometimes there is a conflict between the unspoken reciprocity with their injured kin and the necessary demands of the outside world. The sister of an evidently gifted cerebral palsied boy cannot look directly at the academic future she has promised herself without recognizing both the debt she owes her brother and the pain her absence will cause him.

How can one make judgements about the importance of

214

such reciprocity? The harmony of the world is composed of much that seems contradictory. We can never know enough, so we use other ways to get a grasp of things. These are called symbols. Love, like art, appears to be useless, but could we imagine living without it? The look in someone's eyes, the piece of music, the meal, the conversation, the picture, even our unremembered dreams affect us. We cannot predict when or how much or for how long. In another context, the severely injured child, who lives without hope that hope will reach him in time, struggles on with his life. From the outside we cannot absolutely say such a life is only a burden and should be ended.

A real analysis of the positive aspects of the situation means rather more than a doctor mumbling about 'a lot of happiness coming out of suffering' (as he exits hastily, leaving you with a stiff and screaming child in your arms).

Sibs' moral and ethical dilemmas are endless. While they invariably maintain a fierce loyalty to their hurt sisters and brothers, their views on abortion differ considerably. Pauline Fairbrother spoke to a group who'd all watched a programme about a Down's Syndrome child. His parents had summed up their feelings with the words, 'We wouldn't have him differently.' The mother added that if she knew that she was having another Down's child, she would go ahead. *All* the sibs Pauline spoke to insisted that they would prefer an abortion.

They were basing their judgements on their parents' experience and to relive their parents' lives seemed unbearable. Yet many sibs I talked to had different opinions. Anne, whose brother is Down's, said: 'I would count it an honour to have a child like Mark. Special children need a special kind of parent but I do feel that if *my* child were handicapped I could cope very well.'

Michael, whose sister is mentally handicapped, said:

'Being a Christian I don't believe in abortion. I often think of what I would do. It would come as a great shock to me.'

Garath, whose brother is also Down's, didn't bat an eyelid. 'I've no particular worries whether or not I have a Down's Syndrome child myself. Alex is a great brother, I'd give him a BMX bike if I could afford it.'

But there is a huge diversity of hidden factors. What looks like an alternative to an outsider may well be an impossibility to the family in question. Perhaps no one, not even parents, think through these situations as well as sibs ultimately do. Their formative years are dominated by conflicting values. Nothing comes easily.

Something's lost and something's gained in every life. You can't be the person that your hurt kin makes you without having had them in the first place. Perhaps you wonder what kind of character you would have had without the anguish and the hard work. You may value arriving but regret the scars left by the journey. I imagine many mothers who embrace their newborn infants with joy swear they'll not go through labour again (that is unless they have a greater understanding and control over the processes involved). Thus, being optimistic about the benefit of our experience is rather different from being confident enough to prophesy that we'd repeat the same ordeals given a choice.

The Greek philosopher Solon refused to comment upon whether or not an individual had enjoyed a happy life until after the person was dead. Experience is forever changing experience. Most people need a good fifty years to grasp the state of the game and by the time they see it they are nearly out of it. Not so sibs. In a sense 'life' has already happened to these children who couldn't wait to grow old before they became wise.

The Down's Syndrome baby who hangs tenaciously on to life although she is only receiving water (because the decision has been made that it is more natural to allow her to die) demonstrates the vitality of her organism. Perhaps she has a misplaced optimism in her future (although in her case, given a home treatment programme, the chances are that her disability could be largely overcome). Even the nursing staff admire the child. Nevertheless she is being 'saved' from her own future.

I know that some children are so horribly hurt that death seems as a gift to the beloved. A woman takes into account what society will offer the child. Will it humiliate and exclude the life it exhorts her to save? Will it demoralize her by poverty and privation so that she cannot look after her other children?

The parent of a severely burned and disfigured child once told me: 'There are things worse than death.' Sometimes both life and death are equally frightening. We are all in part responsible for a parent's choice. All of us could have been in this unimaginable position.

An acquaintance of mine had a teenage daughter who received severe head injuries in a car accident. She remained in a coma for weeks. The hospital delicately inferred that death might well be a merciful alternative to 'irreversible' brain injury. Nevertheless my friend continued vigorously harassing her unconscious child until rather grudgingly she woke from her coma. Months later when she could speak the daughter described herself as having been in a long lucid dream in which she repeated her entire life experience in detail. As she reached the day before the collision she began waking up. Returning to the world meant resuming responsibility for a body that was suffering and didn't work properly. It was a hard choice to come back . . .

We do not always know what we want. The mother of a remarkably normal looking Down's Syndrome boy said: 'You need six to eight weeks before you can take a decision about your child. No one should do so on your behalf. The most negative people around me were the medics. When my son went into hospital with a chest infection they wanted to withhold antibiotics.'

The decisions parents take are going to have supreme effects on the nature of their family's survival. How does a mother know what is going to be best for her? Will she cope or will she simply go mad? How much support can she expect from the children's father?

Sibs live at the receiving end. Where theories fade, their daily life begins. Do you remember Pat's remark? 'It was because my mother came out of it that we all came out of it.' By looking after mothers, so the story goes, you provide for children.

In finding ways to help sibs we have to consider realistically what changes can be made, given things as they are. I do not ignore the possibility of a radical approach involving a reappraisal of the social structure, but it is not within the scope of this book to deal with it at any length. We can see that if fathers played an equal role in the home and both parents worked part-time there would inevitably be more crèches and playgroups for all types of children. Given this situation, employers would inevitably become involved.

If your work is unpaid you do it at your own risk. Having children is still officially regarded as almost recreational for women. When the 'recreation' turns into a nightmare as your darling baby rolls its eyes and fits in your arms, you realize what little responsibility society actually takes for the development of the very young. You are the mother, but '*only*' the mother. Without credit or esteem the responsibility is yours to swim, or drown. Architects and planners are not usually women with children. They have co-operated in producing neighbourhoods that isolate women with children. If your child is handicapped, social life is virtually impossible. The more middle class you are, the lonelier it can be. The money that insulates you from deprivation also insulates you from people. The only people who are there to respect your strength because they depend on it are your children.

So suppose we put support for the mother first by creating a situation in which more participation can be encouraged from the father. People tend to rise to what is expected of them if they are given good examples and good moral support. Local authorities need specific departments focusing on the problems that arise in a family when a child is handicapped. (Parents would not then be obliged to confront up to twenty different people in their search for clarification.) Within these departments there could be specific advocates who continue to look after the family's interests from the moment the child's injury is announced to the parents. Ideally, any discussion of the prognosis for the child should be postponed until the advocate arrives to be with the family. The advocate can also talk to both fathers and sibs and arrange for co-counselling with other families. Fathers who have already recognized how much they need to be open and receptive, to cry and to cope, are ideal people to support other men who are still suppressing their feelings.

Sibs, we know, would welcome the opportunity to exchange views with other sibs. As much general information as possible about health, nutrition, rehabilitation, education and so on needs to be carefully studied by the whole family, who have embarked upon a new career for which no previous provision has been made. In such a situation the advocate can pay serious attention to any programme of work that offers a better structure or harmony to the household as well as producing evident neurological improvement in the hurt child. Ways in which the Social Services can help could then be considered and further back-up provided by more crèche and playgroup facilities for hurt and well kids.

There is a desperate need for a 'homemaker' to be appointed by the advocate to offer sympathetic help for the first days or weeks that the baby is out of hospital. These must be understanding people who come into the home for an hour or more each day to give the parent (at present usually the mother) time to rest, let things sink in, and simply to cuddle her children. Her advocate should visit every week and be available on the phone to all members of the household. Phoning up to chat with the other children and meeting them in school is vital. The sibs' school needs to be well primed so that it sees itself as a co-worker on their behalf. This means the co-operation of sibs at home can be assessed as part of their school curriculum and their class assiduously involved. Thus the practical application of caring will become personal to the group.

The advocate should also have enough clout to testify to the family's financial needs before the DHSS. There must, in all fairness, be a change in policy so that recognition is given to how much money parents and sibs are saving the state by the work they do at home. They can then be benefited accordingly. A single parent should no longer be eternally penalized for endeavouring to support her children's exceptional needs, a term which ought to be extended to apply to sibs as well as hurt children.

As hurt kids grow up and are integrated into normal schools, it is important that any separate therapeutic programmes such as those of the Kerland Foundation are respected so that part-time school is not an impossible option but a realistic addition to rehabilitation. It is vital that all the children are taught enough about the problems and the work entailed to ensure that the cruelty which grows out of ignorance and impotence is swept away. The more children are allowed to participate in these matters, the better able they will be to understand themselves and respect hurt kids and their sibs. Where schools are not integrated, special schools and normal schools can 'adopt' each other and the children share as many functions as possible. Possibly special schools will have a more optimistic view of their role in rehabilitation.

By such means it is possible for siblings' experience to be shared by the community. Their classmates will have many opportunities to stand by them when term ends. The advocate is there to see that no family finds itself and its members permanently trapped. To ensure that sibs have the chance to be independent, holidays organized for them need to become routine. When the sibs can hardly be spared, this will simply point to the reality of their Herculean tasks and their advocate can recommend more support to relieve them.

The vital priorities are: no member of the family should have needs that are overlooked; nobody should feel imprisoned or isolated; enough information should be made available; and the family's work on behalf of their handicapped child should be so respected that financial worries do not prevent them getting on with it.

Is it nurture or nature that metamorphoses many of us into carers? Each of us could have been a sib. We can muse upon which factors turn potential young tearaways into the conscientious defenders of their hurt kin. Admiring them is the beginning of a change of consciousness about all children.

So the story ends . . .

'He ain't heavy, mister,' the girl answered. 'He's my brother.'

Watching the couple stagger onwards, the bigger frame leaning heavily on the small shoulder, does the questioner also feel a slight and curious envy before he turns his attention back to his busy life? It cannot be true, for he has everything – but there are things he remains afraid to learn.

Where Are They Now?

As this is being written, Linda, the author, is seventy-nine and maintains an active clinical practice and ambitious ongoing research program at the Advance Centre, a charity she founded in 2002.

Doran, the boy who was never expected to sit up, walk, interact meaningfully with the world, or live much past twenty, is soon to be forty-five.

He walks and has run half-marathons; helps with household chores; paints, shows and sells his paintings; and is a much-beloved figure in his community, engaging in numerous conversations as he runs daily errands in town for his family.

Lili, the subject of *The Other Child*, now forty-six, is the manager of Advance Centre in East Grinstead, Sussex, UK, and has become an expert administer of hyperbaric oxygen therapy. Lili has also become an expert in the unique therapeutic methods Linda has developed based on her decades-long study of neurobiology and many thousands of clinical practice.

Since the founding of Advance Centre, mother and daughter have successfully treated hundreds of children and adults with a wide range of challenges focused on but not limited to neurological disorders: cerebral palsy, multiple sclerosis, autism, seizure disorders, head injuries, Parkinson's, post-stroke, and anxiety disorders.

Linda's work with Doran and many others, ever-supported by

Lili, has been informed over the decades since her authoring of *The Other Child* by high-level collaborations with Carl Stough, the innovative respiratory therapist; Dr. Philip James, a pioneer and the leading advocate for hyperbaric oxygen therapy in the UK; and Professor Patrick Wall, the esteemed British neuroscientist credited, among other things, with developing the gate control theory of pain.

Through Wall's personal intervention, Linda was admitted to the PhD program in Psychology and Neuroscience at the University College London in 1988, despite having had no previous formal training in science.

In addition to the East Grinstead, UK headquarters, Linda and Lili have at various times expanded the practice of Linda's unique therapeutic methods to Germany, Slovakia, Norway, South Africa, Namibia, The Philippines, Scotland and Ireland.

Linda's PhD thesis, "Inquiry into the Possible Influences of Breathing Quality on Outcome in Children with Cerebral Palsy," is the first known comprehensive survey of the scientific literature that documents the connections between respiratory function and the phenomenon of neuroplasticity.

Neuroplasticity is defined by the US National Institutes of Health as "the ability of the nervous system to change its activity in response to intrinsic or extrinsic stimuli by reorganizing its structure, functions, and connections after injuries, such as stroke or traumatic brain injury." In other words, the brain can heal when given the right help and support.

Linda's contribution to the science, amply demonstrated in her thesis and over decades of clinical experience, is documenting the particulars of the role the respiratory system plays in the brain's ability to heal. By fundamentally reconditioning the breathing apparatus of the patient using a method of her invention, more oxygen and much better distribution of oxygen becomes available to the patient which turns out to play a decisive role in the brain's self-healing.

Where Are They Now?

In 2020, the documentary film *Breathe* was released about Linda's work and is available on YouTube and the Advance Centre website. Due to the interest the film has generated in her work beyond the UK, Linda has developed a program for teaching her approach to parents and individuals over Skype or Zoom and now works with clients all over the world.

For more information about Linda's Advance Centre, visit www. advancecentres.com; email: info@advancecentres.com; or call: 44(0)-1342-311-137.

—Kenneth McCarthy

HELPFUL ADDRESSES

UK Charities

Sibs: For Brothers & Sisters UK of Disabled Children
26, Mallard View, Oxenhope,
Keighley, Yorkshire.
BD22 9JZ
Phone: 01-535-645453
email: info@sibs.org.uk
www.sibs.org.uk

Caudwell Children:
Visionary Support for all members of the family with a disabled child
General Enquiries: 0345-300-1348
charity@caudwellchildren.com

Contact: Charity Helpline for families with disabled children
Wenlock Studios
50-52, Warf Road,
London.
N1 7EU
Phone: 020-7608-8700
Email: info@cafamily.org.uk
www.cafamily.org.uk

Scope: Supporting disabled children & their siblings
Phone: 0808-800-333
Email: helpline@scope.org.uk
www.scope.org.uk

Mencap National Centre UK for children & adults with learning difficulties:
Sibs Office
123, Golden Lane,
EC1 YO17
Phone: 020-769-66007
www.mencaporg.uk

US Charities

Federation for Children with Special Needs:
The Centre for Siblings of People with Disabilities
Email: info@siblingscentre.org

Resources to support siblings of children with disabilities (FCSN)
Phone: (800)331-0688
www.fcsn.org

Siblings Support Project
16120 NE 8th St
Bellevue,
WA 98008
Phone: 425-362-6421
Email: info@siblingssupport.org
www.disability info.org

INDEX

227